TOPPER'S TOP TIPS

(The Key to Your Success in Every Exam)

J.P.S. Jolly

DIAMOND BOOKS

Publisher : **Diamond Pocket Books (P) Ltd.**
X-30, Okhla Industrial Area, Phase-II
New Delhi-110020
Phone : 011-40712200
E-mail : wecare@dpb.in
Website: www.diamondbook.in
Edition : 2024

Topper's Top Tips
By - *J.P.S. Jolly*

Preface

This book has been written with one aim and that is to make our readers believe – 'Being a Topper is neither Difficult nor Impossible'. We have tried to describe in simple language, some sure-shot techniques and tips to help you become a topper.

The present age is the age of competition. Hence, it is important for students to adopt newer techniques to have an edge over your competitors. The world is changing every second and one must keep pace with it to achieve desired goals. Revolutionary thinking and embracing the latest technology will help you emerge as a winner in every field.

We are the creators of our destiny and our life is what we make of it. Success joins hands with those who dare and act. If you are serious about becoming a topper, we assure you that you will soon become one. All you need to do is embrace and follow the tips provided in this book.

Although a lot has been written about this topic before, each writer has different things to say and unique style to present his thoughts. The title of 'Topper' is not more a privilege for a special category of students. It is open for all. Each student has the right to prove his skills. Dedication and confidence help students to achieve the goal they have set in their life.

If dealing with metal (iron) can help one become a Tata and trading shoes can help one rise and shine as Bata, you definitely have it in you to become a topper. The key is to believe that if you can imagine achieving a goal, you can achieve it too. Right direction towards education combined with self confidence, will power, and right knowledge for preparation of exams will help a student achieve his goals.

This book will help students get right direction towards becoming a topper. We also hope that you get answers to all your queries about becoming a topper and preparing to achieve this goal.

At last, I would like to express my gratitude towards the honourable Chairman of Diamond Books, Shri N.K. Verma for all the support. Reader's feedback is valuable to me. I would love to hear from you.

I wish all the best to my readers and hope you reach great heights of success in life and be a topper in every exam that you appear in.

With Best Wishes

– J. P. S. Jolly

About the Author

Born on 4th November, 1953, in Meerut district of Uttar Pradesh State, India, Jolly Uncle (J.P.S Jolly) has been immensely successful in carving a niche for himself in the field of writing. This eminent writer has given sterling contributions in the form of about 600 remarkable compositions in leading newspapers and magazines in India.

Jolly Uncle was motivated by tremendous success of his first few literary creations and decided to make a mark in this field. There was no looking back for this talented writer since then.

Jolly uncle believes that each writer has his own style of writing. He had always tried to present his thoughts and tips to readers in a unique way. Being a writer of inimitable calibre, Jolly Uncle's books have always made a mark on readers. His books have helped enlighten the modern society with advanced information and tips on various aspects of life.

According to Jolly Uncle, the sole duty of a writer is not to use heavy words but to use his mental abilities to help readers get knowledge on various topics. A writer needs to work really hard to meet expectations of his readers at all levels. Apart from writing good books, a writer holds obligation towards society.

Hence, special care should be taken to inculcate positivity among readers. His experience in the field of writing has taught him the significant role played by a writer in society. He believes that a writer can bring in a revolutionary change for good with his power of words and knowledge.

Nothing is difficult or impossible to achieve. Jolly Uncle says that with dedication and hard work, one can achieve everything. As a proficient writer, Jolly Uncle has composed many books to inspire his readers. His story books are appreciated nationwide. These books are now being published in different languages including English, Hindi, Punjabi, Bengali, Marathi, Gujarati and many others. Ardent book lovers have appreciated his work and even adopted the valuable techniques mentioned in his books.

Jolly Uncle has been conferred upon with many honours and prestigious awards for his amazing contribution in the field of Indian literature.

– Publisher

Contents

1

You Can be a Topper

Once, a teacher was upset at his student's score in exams. He asked the student to meet him in private.

"So, you wish to be a topper! But you couldn't score a simple question paper. Did you find the questions hard?" the teacher asked.

"Sir.....the questions were easy but.....I faced problems in solving them," the student replied.

"Once you told me that the school management doesn't help you score much despite your efforts in exams. This is not the right thing to say. If you are serious about getting the highest scores in exams, change the way you think. Think positive!" the teacher said.

"Is it possible to become a topper by turning into an optimist?" the student asked.

"Once you are determined to achieve something, nothing can stop you," the teacher explained.

Students want to grow up fast! This is not all. They also aspire to achieve their goals fast. As student, one is attracted to what adults do and their activities. When a student develops strong desire to gain knowledge and work hard, nothing can stop him from becoming a topper.

Education does not have a peak point that can be conquered. Hence, with strong will power and determination, one can reach to new heights of success. This is similar to a kite that catches speed gradually and then flies higher and higher in the sky. Knowledge is the key to a student's success. Adept knowledge and desire to be the best can help any student become a topper.

Experts in the field of education believe that optimism wins 50% of the battle and the rest 50% depends on one's hard work and dedication. Positive thinking is the key element to ensure success in exams. This theory can be better explained by nature's wealth all around us. Here, everything has to start small and weak. One of the classic examples here is that of a tree. It is born from a tiny seed. Small drops of water from river turn into a gigantic ocean. Similarly, focussing on one chapter at a time will help you gain detailed knowledge about a topic.

Patience and dedication are two necessary elements that help a student become a topper. Have you ever noticed a river that is controlled by a dam? Once the dam is removed, it flows fast and smooth. Similarly, eliminating doubts and apprehensions from mind will help you move on to the path of success smoothly.

Friends and acquaintances may try to discourage you by declaring a specific task as 'impossible'. However, it is up to you to believe them or try to accomplish that task with hard work and devotion.

Those who have deep desire to learn and achieve success can seek motivation from a hardworking ant. Success can be achieved by awakening self-confidence within. Students hold immense wealth of knowledge and talent within. Unfortunately, most of them remain unaware of this possession for long.

The major difference between an average student and a topper is not that of power and knowledge but will power. A lot of students waste their time meddling into other's affairs instead of setting goals and focussing on them. They are the ones who regret later on in life.

In case, you face failure in the beginning for some reason, don't lose heart. Simply gather yourself and start ahead afresh. It required many trials before you finally succeed. Fear of failure is the major hurdle faced by students, these days. The fear may attack a student when starting off with a brand new chapter, preparing for exams, or attempting exams. To secure success, it is crucial to try hard to achieve it. Desire to win and trying hard to achieve goal will help you conquer the fear of failure.

Failure stems from pessimism. It is important to develop positive thoughts within and draw inspiration from things around. The sea can be the biggest source of motivation for any student. As a wave hits the shore it breaks and runs out of energy. However, it doesn't stop. It tries several times despite getting crashed and facing hurdles.

What will be the result? This thought stops most students from experiment and trying something new. Success comes from within. Unless a student is confident about his own abilities, nobody can help him succeed. Regardless of the type and level of exam, one must try hard and stay determined to achieve success in it. Will power to win and passion to succeed are important for any student to become a topper.

Students must try and discuss positive things with their classmates and friends. Thinking positive will exterminate negative thoughts before they occupy your mind. Think and feel that something good is going to happen.

I always used to feel that it is impossible to top in exams. However, I tried to kill this thought by an affirmation in my mind, "I'll be a topper; come what may!" Similarly, a lot of students feel that a particular day is not going right. They don't feel like reading books or learning new lessons. However, it is easy to combat this feeling making a strong declaration to yourself – "No matter what; I'll finish off with the lesson, today." Positive affirmations and declarations from time to time will help you emerge as a topper one day.

Miracles and magic don't exist. At least, they don't exist in the dictionary of a topper. Magic doesn't make a topper. In fact, whatever a topper does and achieve is often referred to as magic and miracle. Hence, it is crucial to develop a habit of studying hard right from childhood. Habit of gaining knowledge removes all basic hurdles that one faces during his student life. This way, one doesn't require running behind success. Such students attract success and fame like magnets.

As a student, you must feel, act, and think young. If you fail to demonstrate the enthusiasm found in youngsters, it is quite possible that you would get exhausted and fail way before reaching your final destination. You may agree that a crying baby is an eye sore. On the other hand, a smiling old man wins everyone's heart. So make sure you are always happy and full of energy. Keep a smile on your face and get going.

One question that may have knocked the door of your mind is – 'who will show us the path of success?' Well, these are a lot of sources that can help you in this matter. Right from parental support to the best of teachers and professors, coaching classes, tuitions, and of course the best of schools / colleges, all of these sources help us achieve success in exams. The most admired and accepted source is the World Wide Web. The internet is of great help to students when it comes to gaining knowledge about a specific topic. One can learn about anything under the sun with a click of the mouse.

Library is an integral part of a topper's life. It is a place with thousands of books written by famous writers, playwrights, and poets. Going through these books will provide you with brilliant ideas and tips to move ahead in life and solve serious problems. Most of the philosophical books have revealed that success and dispute are inter-related. Success cannot be solely acquired by wisdom. The secret is 'absolute surrender' of oneself. Surrender of negativity, ego and of thoughts of the past and the future leads to freedom from mental problems such as stress, fears, worries, feelings of guilt and depression. This helps you lead a happy and peaceful life by living in the present and preparing for the ultimate goal. Success in education can be achieved through the following three elements: 1. Repeated Trials 2. Courage 3. Expertise

There is no substitute to hard work. This is what takes a student to the top. Unfortunately, most people only see the succcss of a topper. They don't even try to see the amount of efforts that have gone into it.

Good books help in providing motivation to students. Literature from great personalities inspires them to do their best in life. No wonder books have been referred to as a 'man's best friend'. So make sure you keep a set of good books around you always. The journey to success is best travelled with books. They act as mentors who teach valuable lessons without criticism and punishment.

Success in exams entirely depends on a student and his ability to learn new topics. One must be always ready to start off a new topic and stick to it until one is well versed with each aspect. Success doesn't depend on the number of hours spent in studying but the concentration and hard work one puts in these hours to imbibe required knowledge. Cramming leads to frustration among students especially when appearing serious exams. Hence, it is crucial to understand a topic in depth and prepare oneself with all possible answers to a specific question. As per a famous adage often used by elders, 'one who studies and understands succeeds and one who studies and forgets faces failure'.

Coaching classes and extra tuitions from private institutions has become a rage among students these days. The dependence is so that around 80% per cent students feel that they cannot score decent marks without attending these classes. Although tuitions and coaching classes can make studies easier, they cannot guarantee success. Tuitions are only about giving directions to students and helping them solve problems. However, it is up to students to derive benefits from these classes by working harder.

Each student has a set of shortcomings. However, it is important to either ignore them or improve them. One must never allow these shortcomings to turn into inhibitions. The entire focus should be on spending maximum time studying and learning lessons. Categorising lessons into smaller sections will help students focus on one section at a time and develop expertise in the given topic. It also helps reduce a lot of stress. In case, students encounter with a serious problem, they must seek help from experts or support from parents. They may come up with viable solutions to the problems. The idea is to learn the art of gathering knowledge from everything around us. It is extremely helpful and provides us with a direction to tread on the path of success.

Many students feel that it isn't possible to win over situations and be a topper unless luck favours. They believe in destiny. However, destiny is what one makes of it. It is precisely the result of our efforts. Anyone who studies hard and possesses detailed knowledge about various subjects mentioned in the course curriculum is bound to succeed. Hence, to become a topper, one must keep revising topics unless it becomes a part of one's sub conscious mind. One must have faith in his own skills, capacities, and knowledge to be able to emerge as a winner and carve a niche among hundreds of other students appearing in exams.

Brilliant students always try to use their knowledge and skills to achieve success in life. They are fully aware of the power of determination and self-confidence that helps one reach toughest of goals and aspiration. Hard work and dedication can win over all kinds of problems one faces in life. Intellectuals believe that a battle is either won or lost in mind. If you think you can win, you actually do.

Knowledge is the answer to all kinds of apprehensions stemming from phrases - 'but', 'why', 'how', and 'what'. Toppers spend a lot of their time thinking about new and impressive ways to solve a problem. Cramming up course books alone is not enough to be a topper. One must keep gathering knowledge and enlightening himself with latest techniques to be able to rise above the others.

Several studies and research has gone into knowing the secret of success. Intellectuals believe that only Hard Work can help a student become topper. Here are some of the other components that lead to success.

Top Tips

- One must work very hard to be a topper.
- The secret formula of a bright future is – Right job, right method, at the right time.
- Avoid lying to yourself.
- Hard work leads to success. Idleness is a path of devastation.
- Winning high scores in exams becomes easier by developing self confidence and will power to succeed.

2

Goals and Dedication

Announcement of examinations created a furore among students. Most of them were seen approaching their professors for tips to score highest in the class. One of the professors was amused at the attitude of students of the modern day.

"These children want to reach the top of Everest without climbing on it. Hard work is the last thing on their mind," the professor thought.

Success cannot be achieved without hard work and dedication. Finally, the professor decided to help these students understand the value of setting goals and dedication. Now, the professor asked the students to meet him inside the class. There, he asked one of the students, Aman in the class, "What is the goal of your life?"

"Sir, I didn't understand your question," he said.

"Ok, tell me what would you like to do in future?" the professor asked.

"I want to get married, Sir," Aman replied.

The professor had a hearty laugh and said, "I mean to ask what you would like to become?"

"A bridegroom, Sir," Aman said.

The professor was enraged to hear this.

"Aman, please tell me what would you like to achieve?" the professor got irritated.

"A beautiful wife," Aman explained.

"Aman, what would you like to give your parents once you grow up?" the professor kept on trying.

Aman's mind was revolving around thoughts of marriage. So he said, "A daughter-in-law."

"You fool! What do your parents want?" he asked.

"Sir, they want a daughter-in-law who would take care of them and the house," Aman explained.

The professor asked the boy to sit down. He knew it would be of no use to speak to this boy anymore.

"I wish this boy had focussed more on studies than marriage. This kind of dedication towards studies could have made him a topper," the professor thought.

Now the professor focussed on asking questions to other students in the class.

"So students, what goals have you set for exams?" the professor asked.

The students were surprised to hear this question. This was something they didn't expect. The professor saw the reaction of students and understood that none of the students have set a goal for exams nor they were committed to score well.

"What is a goal? How would you achieve it?" the professor asked the students.

Finally, a student raised his hand to answer the question, "Sir, a goal is something which we want enough that we make an effort to reach it. For example, once, I decided to score 90% marks in exams and made dedicated efforts towards it. With hard work and dedication, I achieved my goal."

The professor was very happy to hear the answer. He tried to explain the value of goal to students.

"All of us work hard but only a few of are able to achieve success. Success comes to those who set a goal in life and work hard to achieve it. Regardless of the size or type of goal we set, it is important to focus on it and try hard to achieve it. Living without a goal is like shooting in the dark. It leads to nothing but waste of time and energy," the professor explained.

"What is life without goals and ambitions? Man without a dream or a vision will ultimately perish. Aim or a goal in life drives one to work hard. Those who don't set goals in life roam about aimlessly and never see the face of success," the professor said.

According to a research conducted, it was revealed that most of influential and successful personalities across the globe believe in setting goals. Upon achievement of a specific goal, they set new goals and work hard to achieve them. This is how they reach new heights of success. So if you wish to be a topper and extremely successful in life, keep setting new goals and achieving them.

Since it takes a lot of efforts and time in setting goals and achieving them, most of the students must be finding this a bit weird. But this isn't impossible. If you wish to achieve big, you must think big.

Experts believe that one must set goals with care. It shouldn't be too big or small. Goals that are too big to achieve can discourage you in the beginning. On the other hand, the goal shouldn't be too small or insignificant that brings only losses for you.

So, how to know about the perfect size of a goal? Here, we would like to say, "Setting eyes on a goal and feet on right path will take you to the desired destination." In short, we must work very hard to achieve goals without boasting about abilities and skills unnecessarily.

Average students spend their time waiting for an opportunity to knock at their door whereas toppers create opportunities to move ahead in life. Let's take it this way. If you enter a building comprising of ten floors with a decision to visit only the fourth floor, you'd never be able to see what the tenth floor looks like and how it feels to reach there. No goal is too distant and no star is too high. It is only as big as you want it to be.

Each challenge in life opens door to many new opportunities. Every goal achieved gives us a new life. Students are bound to face difficulties in their life. Those who know how to deal with them and move ahead emerge as toppers.

When it comes to setting goals, students must focus on some crucial factors. To achieve a desired goal, one must stop day dreaming and start working hard towards the final achievement. If you wish to set a goal of scoring highest score in exams, it is important to work hard at a decent pace to achieve the goal. Regardless of the kind of goal you wish to achieve, it is important to devote your 100% towards fulfilling it. Keeping eyes on goal and walking in the right direction will help you reach the destination soon.

It is not right to think of success in the beginning. Your journey towards a goal should start with an aim to struggle. There may be obstacles, failures, and heart breaks in the beginning. However, you must not be discouraged by these problems. Failure is a part of success and a matter of pride for hard working students.

It is natural to get stressed and face a lot hurdles while on a success journey. Experts in the field of education feel that a student must be happy and stress free to be able to study well. This may be difficult but you must try your best to stay happy and keep a smile on your face. Toppers do the same and this is what distinguishes them from average students.

Many students get affected by negative comments and thoughts of their friends and give up even before trying. This may prove dangerous for your studies and career. So make sure you abandon negative terms such as stress, dejection, failure, apprehensions etc. and embraces phrases like happiness, hope, faith, achievements, success, and many more.

Positive thinking can make a great difference in your life. It will help you achieve your goals and aspirations. Sometimes, we are unaware of our goals and ambitions. This may prove to be a big obstacle in becoming a topper. If at any point of time in life, you feel that you are not clear about what goal to set, simply take help of a partner or your best friend. You may even ask your mentor to guide you for the same.

Students who try hard and fail don't have anything to regret. They should be proud of their dedicated efforts. The real failure goes to those who had never set a goal in their life. One of the secrets of success in a topper's life is that they set a goal, aspire to achieve it, and dedicate their 100% to achieve it.

It is true that some individuals are born genius but following the tips mentioned below will also help one become a genius and achieve success in various stages of life.

Top Tips

- Nothing is impossible for proficient students.
- Dedicated students are not afraid of hurdles coming in their way.
- Dedication, wisdom, and hard work always bear fruits.
- Aspiring toppers should not consider themselves unlucky.
- Obstacles are a part of student life. One who knows how to avoid these or battle these off emerges as a topper.
- Students who keep their eye on the fish's eye and nothing else like the great warrior Arjuna will finally win the battle.

3

Significance of Education

Prior to starting off with a discussion on education and knowledge, it is of utmost importance to understand the significance of education in one's life. Now the question whether one can realise the importance of education by learning course books? Or is it all about gaining expertise in a specific field? To brief it up, education is a legacy which is passed on from one generation to the other.

The power of knowledge and education helps us grow as cultured beings and follow discipline right from childhood throughout life. It also helps us grow and progress at different stages of life. Education is the sole and most powerful source of knowledge available to mankind. It helps one enlighten about a huge range of topics across universe. It helps us edify the new generation and help them lead a happy, healthy, and meaningful life.

Education plays the most important part in a student's life. It is a reliable source for ensuring progress in various fields and key to success for a student. Those who consider it as a means of income may not have understood its real significance in life.

Some students feel that a lot has been said and written about education. Hence, there is no room for writing or explaining things further. However, it is not about the number of times the topic is discussed about. It is about understanding the real significance of education in order to achieve something great in life. Unless a student understands the role of education in life and immense benefits it carries for the future, it is not possible to excel in it and become a topper.

The students of present time are materialistic. They prefer knowing about the benefits of a specific task before undertaking it and making efforts towards its accomplishment. Therefore, in order to motivate them and direct their focus on study, they must be acquainted with the significance of education in life. Although modern students are quite aware about importance of education, some still consider it a waste of time. According to them, studying hard is a waste of time, efforts, and money especially if it doesn't bear fruits. In short, they wouldn't try hard without a guarantee for highest score among their peers. For them, it is all about materialistic gain.

We have a message for our friends who don't consider study an important part of life. Each morning introduces us with a new day and a brand new life. Likewise, Mother Nature undergoes a number of changes frequently. Time is never constant. It changes every second. These changes also have a huge impact on our lives. Society is also going through some drastic transformations every now and then. The field of education is no different. So regardless of the number of times importance of education is discussed, there is still some room left for more. Whether it is about education or achieving success in a desired field, each new day must develop newer, more advanced thoughts within us. In short, education is a reliable source of attracting respect, admiration, and success in life.

The New Age Education

Change of age has given way to advancement in technology and techniques of imparting education to students. Newer and more advanced methodologies have been invented to ensure the best of education to students keeping in mind the demands of modern age developments. Each writer has a distinct style of writing and some special skills that he or she uses to write books and compose other literary works. Toppers are well aware of this fact and use this knowledge for their own good.

Age of Computers

Of course, it isn't fair to discuss modern education without the mention of this iconic machine. Computers are an integral part of present day educational techniques followed in schools, colleges, and institutions. Have you ever noticed that a computer has same answer for a question asked by different students in different style? However, real life is different from the world of computers. When different students in a class ask same question from the teacher, he answers the question according to the capability of each student and their aptitude. Here, the teacher makes sure that all students in the class understand the answer for a question.

Education is the Light of Life

Education is a light that brings the human beings from darkness to light. A single ray of this light can acquaint us with the deepest knowledge about the planet we live in and much more. It is also potent enough to transform miseries of life into happiness. What is the difference between a blind man and one with eyes? For the blind, this world is full of darkness. The man with the eyes sees light everywhere. Similarly, this world is a happy place to live in for the educated and full of miseries for the illiterate. To sum up, education can remove darkness from one's life and fill it with knowledge, happiness, confidence, and wealth.

Education is the Solution of all Problems

Just as the darkness of night is removed by sun, only education can remove problems and obstacles from a student's life. There are times when people are unable to find a lost item in a dark room. Similarly, it is not possible to find solutions to problems without the light of knowledge. Right from a shopkeeper to a labourer working in a factory and a villager knows how important education is and what difference it can make in one's life. Hence, it is extremely important to keep pace with demands of modern world and welcome the light of education in your life.

Education has No Age Limit

A lot of people think that they are too old to learn or attend school. However, this is not true. Losing out on one opportunity during childhood doesn't mean one must close door to other opportunity that comes their way. Education has no limit. Knowledge can be gained at any point in one's life (from birth to death). It is true that time once lost cannot be gained back but you can grab another opportunity to study and start life afresh.

Poor and the Rich – Knowledge is for All

The financial status of the student doesn't matter as far as he is keen on gathering knowledge. Education is equally useful for the rich and poor. It helps one get acquainted with their fundamental rights and even instils ample courage to fight for them too. People across the country are aware of the importance of education. This is also the reason all sections of society, including the poor and rich have their main focus on providing the best of education to their children.

Rule of Utilitarianism

Knowledge can eliminate all kinds of weaknesses and shortcomings in one's life. According to the rule of Utilitarianism, when a man is hungry, the first roti he eats satisfies him the most. Second roti further reduces the level of satisfaction. After a limit, the usefulness of roti is reduced to zero. However, this rule of Utilitarianism does not hold any significance in a topper's life. In fact, they know that the rule works the other way round in a student's rule. A student's hunger for knowledge increases as they gain it.

The world is full of knowledgeable students who talk, preach, and write about knowledge. But only a few become toppers. Those who understand the real significance of education and execute it in their life go on to become toppers. Knowledge shows students the path of truth and helps them emerge as great leaders in their respective fields.

Swami Vivekananda had once said, "Education is the manifestation of perfection already existing in man." According to this great man, education is the sole medium that a student can use to build a prosperous future. Both ethical and intellectual knowledge is important to help a student grow self-dependent. The modern environment demands development of character, brain, and mental strength of students. This is possible only through education.

Education can help us lead the society to path of progress. It helps one develop the ability to distinguish between the right and wrong. One can also keep tabs on various activities and development happening across the globe. Literacy can help a single individual change the society for better.

The importance of education can be elucidated with some powerful examples. A few drops of medicated tonic can do what many cans of water cannot. A small needle can do what a gigantic and more powerful sword can't. Similarly, hundreds of illiterate men are incapable of achieving what a single educated man can.

Students who realise the importance of education in life know that hundreds of winners cannot match up to the glory and power of the 'Conqueror of Destiny' (topper). To be the conqueror of destiny, one must do something different from others and create a unique identity. Let's see what toppers think about the importance of knowledge in one's life.

Top Tips

- Education and knowledge bear sweet fruits.
- Knowledge leads to success.
- Education is a powerful tool. It can change the world for better.
- Right knowledge enhances one's proficiency and helps him become a topper.
- Understanding and following the knowledge provided by books will lead to success.
- Adhering to information provided by education results in success.

4

How to Prepare to be a Topper

As already discussed, setting goals is an important element of preparation for being a topper. These goals will prove to be a powerful source of inspiration for students to score well and achieve desired rank in school / college. A lot of students agree that they would like to become a topper. The only thing that stops them from being one is lack of knowledge about preparation towards achievement of this goal.

We would like to mention an interesting fact about student behaviour. It undergoes a significant change the moment examination dates are announced! Those who wake up late start adhering to alarm clock beep and jump out of bed without constant reminders from family members.

Success in exams depends on both goal setting ability of a student and his commitment to achieve these goals. Concentrating on understanding various topics and sparing adequate time to prepare for exams is also extremely important.

Most students don't set goals for themselves. This proves to be a huge obstacle in the path of success. Without a clear goal, it is not possible to prepare well for exams. Some students have a different perspective towards preparation for exams. We would like to quote an example about a student who was busy with preparations for forthcoming exams in school. One day, his father asked, "How is the preparation going on, my son? There isn't much time left for exams."

"Great, Papa! I have been in the market the whole day searching for the best quality pencils, scales, erasers, and a geometry box. See, I've bought everything. From tomorrow, I will start off with revising the lessons," the boy said.

"I'm not interested in these trivial matters. Just tell me what you have prepared for exams from the course books. Did you remember all of the important topics?" the father asked.

"Papa, I haven't learnt my roll number yet. How can you ask me about course books and lessons?" the boy asked.

The father was surprised at the attitude of his son towards exams. The boy asked, "Papa, please tell me how did you like attending school when you were a child?"

"My son, I liked going to school but studies weren't my cup of tea. I hated studies. Despite doing my best in exams, teachers never used to give me full marks," the father confessed.

"So, that means you never focussed on course books and learning the topics in it well," the child said.

"Well, my son, had I been dedicated to course books and studies, I would have been a topper," the father explained.

Exams are usually a source of panic for parents and students. The environment inside the house is tensed up soon after the student gets his date sheet. Each member of the family seems to be concerned about the one who is supposed to appear in exam. Poor student is not allowed to watch TV, talk on phone, or even listen to music. In case, he is seen indulging in such things, the entire family gets into the preaching mode. However, none of them would tell the child how to prepare to be a topper.

Prior to kick starting studies, it is important to know which way to go. How would you actually start, what would you study first, which topic to give least priority, time required to be allotted for each subject, etc. are some of the significant factors to take into consideration. Each task has a set of rules to be followed. Preparing for exams is no different. Before understanding these rules, you must be clear about the goals and how serious you are to achieve them. Most importantly, you must promise yourself to start off with the preparation without delay. Don't put off until tomorrow what you can do today.

Students of the present age want to reach to the pinnacle of success within a short period of time. However, this depends on how serious one is about reaching the goal. Moving ahead with positive thinking and confidence to achieve goals will help you score well. Staying determined is the key to reach to the top.

With each new class, the pressure on students increases. The course curriculum gets tough and a lot of things need to be taken into consideration. Hence, it is crucial to cement the foundation. So that the student can build a beautiful, strong building over it. The present age is the age of competition. Hence, each student must prepare himself to stay ahead of his counterparts. Nothing should be done in haste. It leads to irreparable losses. Students who don't concentrate on lectures in the class are unable to learn it in a systematic way.

The very mention of the term 'exam' leads to bouts of

nervousness among students. They stop taking care of their health and don't get enough sleep. However, this is not a solution. Here, it is important to stay calm and think positive. Prepare some strategies to rectify your mistakes and avoid making them in future. Manage your time in a way that you get ample time to prepare for each subject in detail.

The next step towards preparing for becoming a topper is to plan a study pattern and set a time table. Planning is the key to success in any task one undertakes. Hence, you must focus on planning your preparation ahead of time. Prepare a practical schedule to be followed in order to cover all of the important topics.

When it comes to acquiring the best scores in exams, most students have a question in mind. All students study the same books, one teacher teaches all, and they all study in the same school / college. Then what is it that makes each student in the class score differently? The difference is in the level of dedication each student has towards reaching the goal.

In order to get higher scores in exam, one must focus on how to study, what to study, and when to study. Study style and quality also plays an important role in obtaining good scores in exams. Style of answering a question also makes a huge difference. The answer is to be clear and to the point.

The best way to solve a question in exam is to be precise and to the point as far as possible. However, most students do just the opposite. They start off by giving an unnecessary introduction and beating around the bush before reaching out to the main point. This wastes a lot of time on the part of student and irritates the examiner. They don't have enough time to read the entire saga and decide on marks after locating the real answer. Intelligent students on the other hand don't believe in wasting time. They give crisp, to the point answers to questions asked. This helps the examiner analyse the student's capacity and the amount of knowledge he or she possesses on a specific topic.

Some students lag behind due to the handwriting style. It is so bad that the examiner faces tough time understanding what is written. Hence, it is important for students to practise writing at home before exams. This also helps in finishing off a specific question within required period of time without compromising on beauty.

Writing down answers on notebooks is the best way to memorise them. It also improves handwriting and speed. Toppers believe in practicing a lot of model test papers. This helps them get an idea on the type of question papers they need to solve and within a restricted period of time.

The style of preparation of exams plays an important role in a student's performance. If you are preparing for subjects like science and mathematics, simply focus on solving different questions instead of repeating a single one again and again. This will boost your ability to solve all types of queries in exams.

Most students find English as the most intimidating subject. We would advise them to prepare for the subject just as they would do for others. Here, the main focus should be on Grammar. Getting hold over English grammar can be tricky. So try reading books of different levels (Beginners, Intermediary, and Advanced) to acquire detailed knowledge about the subject. Experts believe that reading English newspapers is one of the best things to do. This helps a student get hold over the language. Additionally, it provides you with detailed and updated information from across the globe.

In order to gain expertise in a specific subject, it is important to study at least thrice a day. When it comes to preparing for final exams, you must gain knowledge on changing patterns of question papers and stay updated with the course curriculum. To become a topper, you must prepare notes on your own and write on various topics as far as possible.

Just as it is important to see a dream before achieving a goal, you must dream of becoming a topper, set a goal, plan for achieving the goal and work towards it. You need to assess the topics, their level of complexity, and your interests when making a strategy. Also analyse time required to be devoted to a specific topic. Once you have a plan in hand, it is time to execute it.

Being a topper is no less than stretching out hands to grab stars in the sky. You need to work really hard to achieve something as great as this. Think positive and make strategies to be able to tread in the direction of your goal. Every student focuses of studying hard during exams. However, toppers are unique. They have a different style, unique strategies, and perfect directions to achieve what they want. Most of the time the unexpected happens and students who are deemed as nerds in the class emerge as toppers. This is because they don't copy others and focus on minute details of a topic discussed by teachers in the classroom. Toppers are committed to a cause and they do whatever it takes to achieve their goal. Brilliant students discuss topics with teachers and accept their mistakes.

It is important to spend good number of hours in study to become a topper. However, it is not the number but quality that counts. You may spend less number of hours in study but in a constructive way. Mathematics is a complex subject. Instead of learning one formula and using it again and again to solve sums, it is important to look for different ways to solve a problem.

When preparing for exams, take into considerations the type of questions that may be asked. Also get a set of question papers of the previous year and practise it several times. Preparing notes on important topics will help you a lot.

The pressure of exams often discourages students. They don't feel like reading their course books or even talk about them. Lack of interest and focus on studies makes one think a lot about the length, type, and complexity of course. They feel that the course is too big to be handled by their preparations. Here, the important factor is to focus on the most difficult topics and spend more time on it. Dividing each topic into small sections will make it easy for you to prepare each topic with ease. In case, you are unable to pay attention on studies, forget everything. Don't think about how much you need to prepare, the complexity of a topic or the time that is left for you to do so. Simply focus on a topic and think of nothing except finishing it off. Categorising topics into smaller sections will lighten your burden to a significant extent.

Some students are last minute readers. They don't prepare the entire year and roll their sleeves up right before exams. There is nothing wrong to do so if you are capable of complete the entire course in a few months but it isn't the right approach to be a topper. Toppers prepare to achieve their goals right from the first day of session. It helps them complete the course and also leave enough time for rectifying mistakes and revise each topic thoroughly. If you start the race earlier, chances are that you reach the winning line on time.

While it is important to dedicate most of your time to studies, health shouldn't take a back seat. Ignoring health can prove extremely harmful for you. Take special care of your eyes. They get tired and you must provide them some rest. Keep taking smaller breaks and sleep well at night to keep eye related troubles away. Take out some time to enjoy a stroll in the park or play your favourite game.

Don't panic to see the exam dates drawing near. Relax and try to keep stress and other negative emotions at bay. Keep reminding yourself that you have prepared really well for exams and nothing can stop you from being a topper. Self confidence is important to be able to maintain peace and concentration during exams.

Many toppers have admitted that they had never studied more than 5-6 hours in a day. The only thing that helped them was concentration and a peaceful environment. They believe that mind should be in a relaxed state to be able to grasp things faster. Full support from family and teachers works as icing on the cake. Although each student has his own style of studying, we hope that the tips and techniques provided in this chapter will help you become a topper.

Top Tips

- Being a topper is a serious goal. You must take studies seriously and repeat and revise lessons in course books as many times as possible.
- One must exercise control over emotions while preparing for exams. It is as important as learning and memorising lessons.
- Students who stay determined about achieving their goals will become toppers one day.
- Instead on allotting same number of hours to each topic, focus on spending more time on difficult ones.
- Take help from teachers and seniors as and when required.
- There is no secret formula followed by toppers. They simply focus on studying hard, preparing well for exams, and learning from mistakes.

5

How to Avoid Exam Phobia

Exam phobia is a common problem among students these days. The effect is such that students spend sleepless nights agonizing over exams, days, or weeks before they take place. There are many reasons behind this. Some students feel that if a teacher cannot teach all subjects, why is it expected from students (who are less than teachers in all respects) to attain mastery in all subjects. Some also feel that it is not possible to summarise the lessons studied throughout the year in just three hours.

Students face different types of fears during exams. Some fear the capability of their friends, their preparation style, and knowledge while others are not confident about their own capabilities.

Parents and teachers contribute to these fears. They have tons of expectations from students and want them to do exceptionally well regardless of what the situation is. If you live under this fear, then you are not alone. Thousands of students all around the world suffer from this phobia.

The key to ensure success is to battle out this fear and remove all kinds of negative emotions such as depression, anxiety, depression, hopelessness, and despair. Instead, fill yourself with feelings of optimism.

Doubts and apprehensions are the root cause of all kinds of fear. Students are surrounded by fears of failure in exams, scoring less, falling below expectations of parents and teachers, and many more. Here, it is important to keep self confidence high always. Fear is the source of all troubles. It gives birth to nervousness and anxiety.

Once, a husband asked his wife to prepare breakfast early in the morning as he was about to go out on a tour. The wife got nervous and didn't know what to do. She didn't know how to prepare everything so early. The confusion made her add sugar to husband's omelette instead of salt. This was the result of excess nervousness of wife which could have been avoided with a simple planning ahead of time.

Students should never allow fear to overpower their mind and heart. It destroys everything within. Practising prudence is the best way to overcome fear. Problems are a part of life. They come to an end one day. All you need to do is face them with confidence. Life of great personalities such as Lord Buddha, Guru Nanak Dev ji, Lord Rama, and Lord Krishna was full of troubles. However, with confidence, wisdom, and patience, they were able to conquer fear and move ahead in life.

Exams are not the end of world for you. It is an opportunity to get assessed and to prove your ability among thousands of other students. Instead of focussing on negative aspects of exams, think of the benefits. Imagine celebrating your success with friends and family. This will give you strength to avoid phobia of exams.

You must forget about future and all other apprehensions you have in mind. As a student, your duty is towards attaining the goals you have set for yourself. This is what will help you emerge as a topper regardless of what the situations are.

For problems and doubts related to course books, speak to your teachers and take their help. This will help you keep stress and fears away during exams.

Let's see what toppers do to avoid exam phobia at bay.

Top Tips

- Light exercises in the morning and evening will help you refresh your mind.
- Toppers live in present and stay away from fears of future.
- Fear is like a virus that spreads during exams. Hence, you must be careful.
- Fear troubles those who don't work hard or plan well.
- Keep computers and mobile phones away during exams as they create unnecessary stress.
- Avoid thoughts and situations that give way to fear in you.

6

Tips to Boost Memory

Memory, reminiscence, and recollection are some of the most important terms in a student's life. Without the presence of these qualities, it is impossible for a student to even dream of becoming a topper. As a rule, ageing is the most common factor that leads to the problem of weak memory, memory loss, and other related problems. However, the scenario is different today. Immense pressure of studies and expectations from parents and mentors has resulted in memory related problems among young students.

Poor health and lifestyle factors have bad influence on mental and physical health of youngsters. No wonder most students prefer staying awake late at night for studies than rising early in the morning. These habits are giving birth to a number of emotional and behavioural problems such as agitation, nervousness, feelings of pessimism, anxiety, etc. in students. This also has a huge influence on their memory power.

Apart from lifestyle related factors, development in the field of science and technology is also responsible for memory loss among students. This may sound a little strange but it is true that in an attempt to make life simple, people have become dependent on machines and gadgets such as computers, mobile phones, tablets etc. Right from phone numbers to birthdays, anniversaries, special occasions, dates for meeting etc. are stored in computers and mobile phones. These gadgets and machines even give reminders to the owner about various occasions and tasks to be accomplished. So, there's nothing much left for the brain to store or remember. It sits idle the whole day which affects its natural functioning in the long run. Lack of concentration usually leads to gradual loss of memory. One of the best solutions to this problem is focus. Students must focus on studies and spend more time learning and memorising new topics.

As a rule, whatever is forgotten can be retrieved back into memory by knowing the exact reason of forgetting. Reason for forgetting and retain information is the same. Whatever we care for and think about constantly is stored into our memory. Things that we don't think about much are usually forgotten. Hence, while studying, it is important to concentrate on what is being learnt. Now you must be thinking what is there to focus on when you are already learning the topic.

Why are we discussing memory and the problem of forgetting in the first place? There is a special reason behind this. Human brain is designed in fashion to remember what is being shown at present and nothing else. For instance, while watching a movie in the theatre, we get engrossed into the story and forget everything else. A song and dance sequence on the big screen makes us tap our feet. A comic scene makes us laugh and a tragic or serious scene brings tears in our eyes. At this point of time, we completely forget that the movie has nothing to do with real life and connect ourselves with the story completely.

Some of the students have very weak memory. They don't even remember what to be done on a specific day. We know a student who faces difficulty in even remembering whether he had taken his medicine for the day. This is a serious problem and may have a negative impact on one's career in the long run.

Students who face problems memorising lessons usually have trouble in concentrating. A little support from parents, teachers, and friends can help students get over with this problem. God hasn't been biased while distributing brain. However, those who use it right from their childhood gain more knowledge than those who don't use it at all. Making no effort towards learning subjects leads to the habit of idleness and inability to memorise things.

Inability to memorise things is not an illness. In fact, it is a result of lack of alertness of brain. Unless doctors declare any kind of mental or physical illness leading to temporary or permanent loss of memory, it is not wise to admit that you suffer from an illness.

Any task undertaken with complete focus and alertness can never fade from memory. This is also true in case of a task that is carried out for the first time. If you have learnt to ride bicycle in childhood, you must be aware how difficult it is to handle it. Similarly, when we learn to drive car or scooter for the first time, the entire focus is on the road. We fear accidents and take care of everything from clutch to breaks, steering, indicator, etc. On the other hand, after gaining expertise in the task, it is easy to drive vehicles while gossiping with friends. The same theory is applicable in studies. Learning a subject light heartedly and by enjoying the contents will help you remember things for a long time. However, a little error from our side may lead to problems. Hence, it is important to focus on accomplishing given course with care.

Here, we will mention some tips to improve memory and get rid of all problems related to memory. Most of the time what students refer to as weak memory is actually not a health condition. This is similar to a situation where we forget something at home and after a few months when we need it, we are left with nothing. Sometimes, you may even forget name of your friends.

One of the classic examples of weak memory is a common instance faced by many of us. There must have been times when you left for home with your friends and forgot to stop at your desired destination i.e. your home. This is because you were engrossed in chat with your friends that you couldn't focus on your desired destination – the home. The same thing happens while learning lessons in school or home. Since you don't concentrate well on books, nothing gets stored in your memory for long.

Just as exercise is important to keep body healthy, regular practise and focus will make your brain more alert. This enhances memory power. Some of the best exercises for brain include solving puzzles and crosswords in magazines and newspapers. Playing special video games (mind power) is also very helpful. These activities help in improving memory.

Most students find it very difficult to recall answers to questions asked in exams. On the other hand, it is impossible to erase memories of being thrashed by a teacher a few years ago. This is because human mind remembers what it wants to and forgets everything else.

Students who score very high marks in exams try to concentrate while learning a specific topic. Their prime motive is to record each word into their brain to remember it forever. In case, they face some difficulty in learning a specific topic, they simply write it many times. These students work really hard to memorise each chapter and revise it several times.

Toppers know the philosophy of success and failure – It takes many years of hard work to reach to the top and only a few minutes to reach the bottom. Hence, they do everything that is possible to achieve a position they desire and work harder to maintain the position. They are also aware of the importance of revising a specific topic again and again. The practise session helps boost memory and remember everything for a long time.

Some students complain about their teacher's habit of asking students to revise a topic several times. They find this task extremely boring. In fact, the teachers emphasise more on writing part which is quite difficult and eats up a lot of time.

Students of modern age also feel that the present education pattern is unfair keeping in mind a student's capacity and time available to study. They also feel that if one teacher cannot teach all subjects why it is expected from students to gain expertise in multiple subjects. Well, this is an interesting topic to discuss but without a solution. The present age is of competition and specialisation. But by studying multiple subjects, a student is getting opportunity to gain knowledge on a wide range of subjects.

If you have decided to become a topper, it is important to start focussing on studying and learning lessons. Students usually spend good amount of time playing out in the field without getting bored. However, when it comes to studies, the mind gets distracted to a number of things such as games, computer, social media, and many more. This may lead to losses in the long run.

Make sure you don't keep television, radio, mobile phones, and computers on while studying. It is better to turn the mobile phone off or in silent mode while studying to avoid unnecessary distractions. Also make it a habit of preparing notes on important points of a topic while learning lessons. This will be helpful while revising topics during exams.

Usage of computer and internet should be restricted to extracting important information. Unfortunately, most students use computer for accessing social networking sites which wastes a lot of your precious time in chatting with friends.

Display boards can prove to be an important tool for students to memorise difficult topics. Although these boards are used in schools, students can buy one for home to record important things on it. In case you are unable to learn a specific formula or answer, simply pin it up on the board. Looking at it again and again will help you memorise it easily. The board can be used for many other purposes such as writing goals, inspirational quotes etc.

Apart from memorising new lessons, it is important to revise what has been taught in the past. This will help you memorise the entire course well. Remember that anything that stays out of sight goes out of mind too. So it is better to spare some time and revise the topics from the past.

One of the most common examples to prove the 'out of sight out of mind' theory is a situation where people buy things from the market which they don't need at present and shove it somewhere in the closet. After a few months when it is time to clean the almirah, they get to see what has been stored in it for long. This is because one remembers things that move around their eyes and forget once they go out of sight. Students who understand this philosophy and keep in regular touch with topics mentioned in course curriculum don't face problems during exams.

Toppers also understand the benefit of studying early in the morning. Most students are capable of accomplishing several topics within 2 hours early in the morning. On the other hand, the productivity is reduced by half during the day. How is it possible? There are many reasons behind this. Your mind is fresh and in a peaceful environment early in the morning. On the other hand, there are many distractions during the day. Studying early in the morning helps one record everything in mind, just like a computer.

No student will ever work hard if there is no fear of result. However, those who aspire to be a topper must focus on studying really hard, memorise each chapter well, and understand its significance. As already discussed, writing helps students remember things for a long time. The practise is time-consuming but gives tremendous results.

Many parents feel that their child is suffering from weak memory and hence, remains unable to fetch marks according to the efforts he or she makes. They feel bad about their child staying awake the whole night and still remain unable to fetch decent marks. On the other hand, there are students who study only for a few hours and score well. The reason behind this is lack of concentration. Parents must stop comparing their children with others. They must support and help children improve their concentration levels.

Scientists and researchers believe that most of the part of human brain is asleep and only a small portion is alert. Topics that we are unable to remember despite several attempts actually get stored in the part of brain that's asleep.

Household environment also plays an important role in one's memory. The best time to kick start study is when the mind is at peace. Tensed up environment at home can have adverse effect on one's ability to study and memorise. Some students remain unsuccessful in scoring well in exams due to stress and tensions at home. It becomes very difficult for them to concentrate on studies.

There are some students who take help of medications, drugs, and energy drinks to boost their capacity and memorise without difficulty. However, this is not the right approach. Over the counter medications can have negative impact on health in the form of serious side effects. According to medical experts, there is no drug or chemical combination that can boost one's memory power. The only thing that works is a winning combination of healthy diet, adequate sleep, regular practise, and hard work.

Human body works as a machine. Using a machine continuously without rest in between can result in breakdowns and other flaws. On the other hand, giving small breaks and rest to the machine keeps it in good condition for a long time. Our prime motive behind quoting these examples is to help you remember it for a lifetime. Whether it is about studies or relaxation, students must take care of time restrictions. Each activity must be conducted, keeping in mind the value of time.

According to a research, it has been proved that those who remain under constant stress and anxiety suffer from weak memory. Just as 6-7 hours of sleep is necessary to ensure apt rest for body, one must give rest to brain and eyes. After studying for long hours, the body requires some rest and sound sleep.

Students who think studying for long hours with complete dedication will not create miracles, they are wrong. Each day of a student should be started with a well planned schedule. An average student uses only 15-20% of brain in his lifetime. To be successful in life, one must focus on look back and understand the mistakes made in the past. Also avoid repeating the mistakes made in past.

If you aspire to become a topper, try and develop your thinking in a unique manner. This also means that you should be able to start off with difficult topics at first and then proceed to the easier ones. Try to wake up early in the morning and revise lessons in fresh peaceful environment. This is the best way to store information in your mind for long.

"Honhaar Birban Ke Hot Cheekne Paat" – The seedling that is capable of growing has shiny leaves. This famous adage holds big amount of truth. Toppers are not made in a single day. They have been working hard and practising since childhood. These students develop a habit of learning things fast resulting in sharp memory and wit. They are also successful in memorising complex topics without difficulty.

One of the best ways to fight out memory related problem is to revise at least 2-3 times whatever has been learnt for the day. Although there is no rule set for the number of times one must revise a specific topic, not revising at all can increase the risk of forgetting major topics in the long run. Toppers have impressive memory power. Let's see what makes it possible for these brilliant students to memorise so much and attain an enviable position in the class.

Top Tips

- Start off with your favourite topics to boost memory power. If you feel you are losing interest in a specific subject, simply stop forcing yourself into it and take a small break.
- Regular practise can help sharpen memory and brain power in the long run.

- Toppers prefer waking up early in the morning to study than staying awake at night.
- Successful students believe in studying each topic with full concentration and interest. This style of studying is helpful in storing details of each topic into memory.
- In order to memorise a specific name or fact, try to picture an image which closely relates to it. This will help you remember it for a long time.
- Toppers take good care of their nutrition and health. They also take care of getting at least 6-7 hours of uninterrupted sleep daily. Lack of good nutrition and sleep can have negative influence on one's memory.

7

Simple Techniques to Become a Topper

Have you ever come across a student who doesn't want to become a topper? We are not talking about whether he or she would like to make efforts towards it. This is just about a desire. Every student across the globe would like to be a topper and emerge as a hero of the class, college, or university. After all who doesn't like fame and admiration? However, only a few are aware of the foolproof tips and set of skills required to achieve this goal. In short, most students don't know how to prepare for the same.

As per a common notion among people, God favours some individuals and toppers are one amongst them. However, this is just a myth. God has created all human beings as equals and blessed with same set of skills. It depends on us entirely to discover innate skills and use them for our own good. However, simply discovering a talent within won't work. The real effort will start thereafter. One must enhance, sharpen, and use that skill wisely.

Some people think that only the elite class of society can afford to send their children to the best of schools in city and become toppers. However, prior to thinking about such things, it is important to know that poverty is no sin. In fact, it is the greatest blessings one can have.

Whatever you wish to achieve in life, you are capable of doing just that. These magical powers are present in each student of today. As already discussed, one does not require belonging to any specific category. It is all about working hard and dedicating oneself to the goals devised.

Toppers are not born from a specific section of society, each one of us has the ability to score well in exams. So, if you are looking forward to win the race, all you require doing is study hard and dedicate yourself to the goal set by you. Another most important thing to keep in mind is the pattern of study. You need to keep it simple by paying attention to each lesson and topic taught by your teacher from the first day of school or college. Panicking at the last moment during exams will only lead to stress and related problems. Also keep a record of notes and worksheets with you to avoid last minute rush during exams.

One of the major problems faced by students these days is revising lessons again and again. Reading a lesson for the first time seems to be interesting. Second time, the interest on the subject is reduced to half. Third time, the entire practise becomes extremely boring. This is owing to repetitions that the student loses interest in it.

Toppers keep themselves away from all kinds of negative emotions. They aren't bothered by the level of complexity of a subject or doubt their own ability to accomplish it successfully. The task of studying course books is not a fashion for these students which they get bored of. In fact, they consider it as a challenge that must be taken and won at any cost.

Most students agree that being a topper is a tough game altogether. After all, one must do something exceptionally good to achieve an extraordinary goal. Hence, to reach to the top, it is crucial for students to forget about momentary pleasures and luxuries. Their eyes should be set only on their goal. Students who dedicate themselves to books are the ones who get to the top.

When starting off with lessons at the beginning of a session, students may have many apprehensions in mind related to how they would fare in exams or whether they will actually be able to cope up with the pressure. However, toppers only focus on the positive aspects of their session and ignore any such thoughts that disturb them in the course of time. Positive approach towards life attracts support from all sides.

Language and expressions are an integral part of every exam. To be able to succeed, one must conquer their mind and heart. Success will not knock at your door. You must make efforts and travel a specific distance to achieve it. This is similar to the story of a bird who must leave his nest, fly up in the air, and search for his own food.

Criticism is a part of success too. Unless a student is criticised for his work, it may not be possible to bring out the best in him. Disapproval and rejection helps one get acquainted with his flaws and disabilities. It also gives one, a chance to improve for better. Each student must face a set of difficulties and troubles during his lifetime. However, with determination, positive approach, and will power, one can easily overcome these and move on to become a topper.

These days, students are exposed to a huge number of facilities and support systems that make their journey, a smooth affair. The sources are good enough to help students clear any exam without much trouble. Unfortunately, clearing an exam is not enough for students, in the present world. Scoring fewer marks can be worse than failing in an exam. This creates a negative impact on a student's career.

Each task has a set of rules attached to it. Preparing for exams is no different. Here, one must take things seriously and employ some smart strategies. Not planning well may lead to a lot of problems during exams.

Now, let's focus on some expert tips that will help you reach to the top. Experts in the field of education have some special tips for students. According to these reputed personalities, it is crucial for each student to set a goal and work hard towards reaching it. Studies are no less than strict penance a student must follow. Here, the focus should be on gaining literary knowledge, practicing positive approach towards life, fighting off adverse situations, and displaying courage to ensure a smooth journey to the final destination.

Time is your Best Friend

When it comes to scoring exceptionally high marks in exams, time is your biggest support. Correct usage of time will help you gain adept knowledge in required amount to be able to ensure success.

Focussing on Minute Details

This is precisely what toppers do when it comes to attending classes. They pay full attention to what the teachers say and try to understand the topic well. These students don't ignore even the smallest and the most insignificant sections of a topic. Nothing is 'already known' to them. In fact, toppers believe in learning each topic well and with a new perspective despite the amount of knowledge they already possess. Dedicated students take notes in the class and record important points to be able to revise during exams.

Homework

Nothing is better than studying a topic in detail while preparing for exams. This becomes easier if a student focuses on doing his homework regularly and on time. A detailed schedule will help you concentrate on studies better.

Nothing is Insignificant

One of the major differences between a topper and an average student is commitment towards each topic. For toppers, the word 'insignificant' doesn't really exist. They concentrate on everything that is taught unlike their counterparts who jump on to the 'main' sections of a lesson. This attitude leads to serious problems in exams. A small twist and little complexity added to the test paper make it difficult to solve for an average student. No wonder toppers reach an enviable position which appears to be an unachievable goal for their classmates.

Solve it on your Own

There are some subjects that demand exceptional attention from the student. Some of these include science and mathematics. In order to get a hold of these subjects, you must try and solve the questions on your own. This develops deep understanding about a specific topic which is extremely helpful during exams.

Keep a Record of your Notes

Notes hold a great significance in a student's life. These are as important as your course books. So make sure you keep a record of these notes and keep revising them as often as possible. Notes are often summarised versions of a topic to help students keep a track of course. Revision of these notes during exams is quite helpful.

Coaching Centres / Tuition

If you are attending separate coaching classes for preparation, it is important to keep the notes provided by the classes in a separate file. Also keep other materials provided by the centre to be able to access them as and when required.

Develop Interest in Complex Topics

There are times when students are unable to develop interest in a specific topic initial. Gradually, the topic becomes an eye sore and a matter of ignorance. However, complexity of a topic and boredom factor attached to it is in your mind. You must make efforts to remove the blockage and start enjoying the topic. The idea is to stop thinking that a specific topic bores you. If at first, a topic gets on your nerves, simply start giving it more time, and take it as a challenge. Divide the topic in sections and start focussing on a very small section at a time. Take help of your mentors and conquer your fear.

Practise Makes One Perfect

Being a topper isn't a cakewalk. Regular practise of a specific topic is what will help you reach to the top. Hence, it is not wise to ignore the power of revision.

Developing Special Skills

There are some special skills one must develop in order to become a topper. Here is a list of what aspiring toppers must focus on.

Top Tips

- Direction is more important than speed.
- Hope, faith, and unwavering confidence is what it takes for a student to get to the top.
- Solutions and not problems aspiring toppers must focus on.
- Being a topper seems to be an impossible task only until you start making efforts towards it.
- Fear of failure is the biggest obstacle in the path of success.

8

Positive Visualisation

Prior to understanding what Positive Visualisation is all about; let's know how it impacts the life of a student. We'll also throw light on its significance and benefits. According to intellectuals, one is successful if he has obtained high level of education. On the other hand, one who has maintained a positive attitude towards life and under the harshest of situations is referred to as the most successful person. Positive visualizations usually refer to using the imagination to create a desired scene. It is a stage where one's mind, brain, and heart are in unison. Successful students agree that positive thinking can help one achieve everything he or she desires for. It leads one to the path of success and helps in achievement of goals in life.

Now the question is how can positive visualisation help a student? Well, this fact is supported by a theory that a student must feel happy, hopeful, and be devoid of stress and apprehensions. One must develop immense amount of faith within to learn a specific topic and acquire enough confidence to train others.

Developing positivity within will fill a student with enthusiasm and energy.

Students with positive perspective towards life are very confident and hopeful individuals. They have full faith in themselves and are quite hopeful for their future. This is also the reason they always talk about success and achievements. Such students are not afraid of results regardless of the kind of goals they set for themselves. The power of positive thinking gives them the confidence to achieve the toughest of goals in life. So if you are preparing to be a topper, simply think, feel, and breathe positive.

Positive visualisation is powerful enough to make a student's journey easier and pleasant. No wonder it is also known as the Success Mantra. There are many examples in the past that reveals the secret behind successful personalities. These individuals tried to accomplish great tasks that were impossible to be undertaken. Confidence and optimism helped them achieve these goals and secure a winning position.

A lot of students don't agree with their professors when they offer lectures on positive visualisation and optimism. For students, these are bookish philosophies that don't see the light of day under adverse situations. Well, these students cannot be blamed. The present world is loaded with negativity. People are living with miseries and feeling of hopelessness. Additionally, immense pressure of studies has forced them to feel negative about everything.

Not only students but adults and seniors with vast experience in every aspect and phases of life feel this way. The slightest of doubt gives birth to thousands of negative feelings within. Here, students must focus on keeping away from stress and negative emotions and focus on studies. Nothing works out without confidence and hope.

Researchers feel that an average student is surrounded by hundreds and thousands of negative feelings whereas toppers are capable of converting all of these emotions into positive. It is true that a student requires facing huge number of hurdles in their lifetime. However, it is not wise to get affected by these problems and give up. Just as for every lock there's a key, every problem has a solution. All you need to do is find the solution by using the power of positive visualisation.

You must have observed a simple theory being followed at homes. Sending water from bottom to top is a difficult task. On the other hand, it is easier to do it the other way round. Keeping this theory in mind, moving ahead in life with positive attitude may be a little difficult but it works really well in the long run.

Conversion of negative into positive is a challenging task and involves a lot of considerations to make on the part of students. Prior to conversion, one must find out the root cause of negative emotions. How do they invade your mind and when? Knowing this will help you exterminate each source of negative thought. This way, it is possible to stay away from everything that keeps you away from confidence and positive thoughts. When each negative thought is turned into positive, no student will consider becoming a topper, an impossible task.

Once a student gets trapped into the cycle of negativity, it is extremely tough to come out of it. When encountered with an adverse situation, simply think of it as a test that you must pass with flying colours. You must find a way out. Positive thoughts and visualisation can help you under these situations. Optimism can help students deal with stress and keeping troubles at bay.

In case, you are unable to attempt an exam successfully, don't worry. One exam will not devastate your life. Life is too big to cry over an exam that goes wrong. All you need to do is focus on other exams and prepare well.

According to researchers, once a student's mind is occupied with negative thoughts, 95% of his innate capacity to study well is destroyed. So now you know how bad an impact negative thoughts have on one's life. These are the biggest enemy of one's life. Hence, intelligent students always prefer taking help of positive thoughts to move ahead in life. As a result, they move ahead in life and spread happiness around them.

Toppers admit that positive thinking helps one remain hopeful and confident about results. Dedication is important to achieve desired results under all conditions (regardless of how adverse they are). Courage is one of the biggest powers human beings are blessed. It can transform one's course of actions drastically. Positive thinking can definitely help any student become a topper.

Now that you know the importance of positive thinking, you would like to know how to develop it as well. First, it is critical to understand that one doesn't hold control over others and their feelings. It is just about oneself. Hence, one must look for potential within to develop positive feelings. This helps one face all kinds of adversities and secure success in life.

Here, we would like to mention an interesting situation to support this theory. Let's imagine it is raining outside. Now it is not in your hands to stop the rain. However, you can take an umbrella and move out of home without being affected by rain.

Most of the time, we look for solutions to the problem outside without knowing that these are usually available within us. All of the problems in life except illnesses, birth, and death are a result of one's own actions and imaginations. Hence, the solutions can also be found within. As you realise your weaknesses, you will develop fresh positive thoughts within.

Students must face all situations with positive attitude and try to solve problems as soon as possible. Your perspective towards life is your best friend. It is impossible to develop a feeling of optimism without changing your perspective towards life. Positive thinking is the stepping stone to success.

Optimistic students usually get the best of opportunities in life. They achieve goals with ease, one simply need to integrate positive visualisation as an integral part of life. The practise will take them ahead on to the path of success.

Although many students work hard towards achieving their goals, only those with distinct style can get to the top. It is rightly said, - 'one who believes he has lost, loses everything and one who believes he has won is the winner in true sense'. So once you set a goal and start making efforts towards achieving it by following the rules of positive visualisation, half the battle is won. Most importantly, it is crucial to change one's perspective towards life.

The only thing you sometimes have control over is perspective. You don't have control over your situation. But you have a choice about how you view it. It is similar to turning pictures to watch it from another perspective. Change of perspective will change the situations around and a change in direction will change destiny.

These amazing secrets are valuable for any student who aspires to become a topper. So why not integrate them into our life and climb the ladder of success!

Top Tips

- Make friends with happy, cheerful, optimistic individuals.
- Positive thinking leads to success and enough scores to help you become a topper.
- There is only a thin line difference between toppers and average students. It is the positive approach towards life that distinguishes toppers from others.
- Change comes from within. So try and bring a positive change within.
- The ladder that takes one to the top is narrow and reserved for only a few. So it is not possible for many students to climb together.
- Being a topper isn't easy. The journey is full of challenges.
- Haste makes waste. It leads to awkward situations for students.

9

The Success Mantra

Once you see a dream, it is time to pave way to fulfil it. Toppers are different from others. Hence, to reach your destination of being a topper, you have to be different and do things differently. Don't take a road that everyone else is walking on. This will only make you a part of the crowd. To emerge as a topper, you must rise above the crowd and carve a niche of your own. Success is achieved through hard work. Everyone knows it. However, only a few know which direction to work on. Those who do, become toppers. Some students are pessimists and spread negative thoughts all around. According to them, a lion sleeps for 20 hours in a day and is still the king of jungle whereas a donkey who works hard is often beaten and cursed by his master.

Well, before quoting these examples, one must understand the difference between protagonists. Animals are different from human beings. They are leading life the way they have been many centuries ago. A lion was a meat eater decades ago and is still one. Cow was a grass eater and is still one. However, this is not the case with human beings. They lived in jungles many centuries ago and today, they have reached Mars. This is a classic example of human success.

Each one of us nurtures a deep desire within to score brilliantly in exams and impress our elders. However, the dream also makes us realise competition with many contenders who are ready to compete with us. Now the question is who would finally win? Since there are hundreds of candidates vying for a single position, it is natural for a student to think that it all depends on destiny. Is it true?

Well, many students feel that working hard for a few days (before exams) and studying like everyone else is enough to be a topper. If that was the case, there would have been hundreds and thousands of toppers in every city. Unfortunately, this is not so. There are only a few toppers among thousands of students who appear in exams each year.

Teachers and professors always advise students to work really hard to achieve the highest position in class. And this is where most students fail. They study for 2-3 hours in a day. Their focus is on everything around except studies. Have you ever thought seriously why only a few remain successful? The answer is simple. Others have not tried as hard as they should. They haven't tried as hard as they do to search for their mobile phones early in the morning. Imagine a situation where someone snatches your purse and runs away. What would you do? Would you stop to put on your best sneakers to run behind the thief? Would you stop by at a juice corner to relax and gain some energy? Would you stop to say hello to a friend who you happen to meet on the way? No. In fact, you will run faster and harder without rest until you catch the thief. This is exactly what the toppers do. They don't rest until they reach their destination.

Different people have different things to say about achieving success in life. Once, a political leader was interviewed by a journalist.

"Sir, what do you attribute your success to?" the journalist asked.

"Taking right decisions at the right time," the leader gave a prompt answer.

"Sir, can you please give us some tips on taking right decisions?" the journalist continued.

The leader smiled and said, "It isn't easy, my dear. The skill comes with experience."

"And how do we get this experience?" the journalist asked.

The leader was left with no choice but to say, "By taking some wrong decisions."

To err is human. Students are no different. All you need to do is learn from mistakes and avoid repeating them. Repeating mistakes can be extremely dangerous for your future. When you see success through the eyes of an optimist, it appears as a straight line. This line works as a Laxman Rekha between success and failure. Lakshman Rekha, in modern Indian parlance, refers to a strict convention or a rule, never to be broken. It usually refers to the ethical limits of an action, traversing which may lead to undesirable consequences. Hence, it is important to avoid crossing this line.

Success comes to those who dare and act. The weak never get a chance to taste it. Challenges are a part of student life. One must face these to emerge as a winner. Beauty comes from pain. Gold must go through fire before getting shaped into attractive ornaments. The finest diamond must be cut before it becomes the most valuable gem. A rock is transformed into an idol after it is cut and refined by an artisan. Human beings are no different. They must develop and enhance exceptional skills to be able to reach to the top.

A topper is never afraid of obstacles he faces in life. He holds on to the hope and keeps treading on the path of success. They know that hope is a thing with feathers that help them fly high regardless of the situation around. With hope, one can cling on to a goal despite facing biggest of hurdles.

Success depends on what you do and how much you do. You must keep trying and working hard to achieve your goals. Toppers always believe in 'doing something great' while an average student wait for 'something great to happen'.

Some students remain unable to reach to the top because they don't take opportunities seriously. It is only when one stretches hand and grabs opportunities that they can taste the fruit of success.

Apart from learning and following the mantras of success, one must also focus on self assessment. This reduces dependency on others and helps in acquainting one with his strengths and weaknesses. Self assessment can reveal your personal attributes, values, skills, and interests, all of which are critical in helping you make informed career choices. However, most students are afraid of self-assessment. This is because they fear facing their own flaws and disabilities. Fear is the biggest enemy of man. Fearing failure can keep one away from a lot of opportunities in life. Failure shouldn't be feared. It should be faced and battle out. So try and try till you succeed. Don't be discouraged. It is often the last key that opens the lock.

Securing first rank in an exam is not difficult once you are determined to do so. All you need to do is keep polishing and enhancing your knowledge and skills. Some students may find this a little difficult to follow but having an unwavering resolution in place will help overcome all obstacles. Besides being brilliant students and hard workers, toppers are humble beings. You must practise modesty to achieve success and respect among people around you.

Let's pledge to adhere to the above mentioned rules to reach to the top and integrate the following golden points in life.

Top Tips

- Being a topper is no rocket science. Any student can become a topper with hard work and dedication.
- Passion is a necessary element to achieve something great in life.
- Positive thinking and rock solid determination leads to success.
- Complete surrender not wisdom alone that helps one achieve success.
- Brilliant students face problems and make ways to fight them off.
- Future is a dream, forget it. Past is bygone, let it go. Present is a gift, use it, cherish it, and enjoy it.

10

Time Management

Modern age students are well versed with the latest technologies and inventions including the internet, mobile phones, and other gadgets. They also keep tabs on each second that passes by. It would not be wrong to say that they know and understand the significance of time management. Most importantly, they know how valuable time is. However, it is still important to be aware of the actual definition of 'time management' to be able to incorporate it into your life.

Time Management can be defined as the ability to plan and control how you spend the hours in your day to effectively accomplish your goals. Students must learn how to manage their time in order to do the best with the time that they have. This helps in accomplishing course curriculum on time and achieving desired results.

Living without a Clock!

The most fundamental rule of time management is to avoid access to clock as far as possible. Experts in the field of education feel that only weak and irresponsible students like to keep an eye on time at study table. Sincere students simply focus on learning lessons and accomplishing the given tasks.

Each Second is Valuable

Only those who understand the significance of time can achieve success in life. Each second is precious and must not be wasted in insignificant tasks. Toppers utilise their time wisely.

Time Wasted is Lost Forever

Only toppers know the importance of time. They are also aware of the fact that lost time cannot be regained. Hence, they try really hard to keep pace with time in hand and utilise it in gaining knowledge and related activities.

The Topper Time

A lot of students want to know the precise number of hours they must spend studying to be able become a topper. Well, this is a tricky question. It depends on one's capacity to learn and understand a subject. For instance, some people take just 15-20 minutes to read a newspaper completely. On the other hand, it takes more than 3 hours for another individual to read the same newspaper. Similarly, it depends on a student's capacity to decide on the number of hours to devote to studies. The number of hours devoted should be enough to help a student understand a subject well.

Time is Life

Toppers know that time is life. Time should be spent on learning and filling mind with constructive things. Time is the biggest mentor and the most powerful element in a student's life. Health experts and doctors across the globe have invented ways to treat various diseases. They have even developed machines and organs that can replace natural organs in one's body in case of organ failure such as a heart, pacemaker, kidney, liver, etc. However, they have been unsuccessful in inventing something that can replace blood. Scientists have also not been successful in replacing time or holding control over it. This is also the reason time is valuable and one must not waste it in any case.

How to Develop Time Management Skills

This is an important skill to develop for a student especially if he or she aspires to become a topper. Now the question is how to develop it. Suppose a classroom comprises of 50 students. Most of the students are capable of securing 60-70% marks in exams. Others have to toil really hard to score about 80-90% marks. Only 1-2 students in the class are capable of reaching to the top. So, what is the reason behind this? All of the 50 students are studying in the same school, same class, and being coached by same instructors.

This is simple. The teacher has played his part in showing the right direction to the students. Now it is up to the students to understand these directions and tread on to the path of success. It is a race. One who starts early and completes the journey reaches to the top.

Many students don't pay heed to what teachers teach in the class. They waste their time in insignificant activities and ignore studies. But as exam draws near, these students regret on mistakes they made in the past and it gets too late to prepare for scoring the best marks.

There are only 24 hours in a day. Eight hours are spent in school/college and travelling. Another 8 hours are spent in sleeping. Now it is only 8 hours that one is left with. Time management is all about utilising these 8 hours resourcefully. A student must focus on exploiting these golden hours into their fullest.

The Difference

There is certainly a huge difference between toppers and mediocre students. Toppers have only one thing in mind – the course curriculum. The topics are on their mind even when they are walking in the park, swimming, or in the gym. Books travel with them always. In short, books are the central part of their life. This way, they are never out of touch of their course.

Prudent Usage of Time

Time is arguably our most valuable commodity. It is not possible to collect, earn, or hoard it. Money cannot buy it. It slips away and nothing in this world can bring it back. So use it or lose it. Saving time is the best way to use it. Students who develop a habit of finishing off tasks on time are usually successful. This is precisely where time management comes into action. Students must prepare a timetable for the next day in which they should mention all of the activities to be undertaken the next day. Preparing a strategy and managing time will help you give exams without difficulty.

Time Management isn't Easy

Students usually find time management as a troublesome task. This is because they aren't really excited about studies. The very mention of term 'study' evokes a feeling of ennui in them. On the other hand, toppers don't mind thinking about, speaking about, writing about, and preparing about studies.

The Art of Saying No

Toppers in school and college are fully aware of activities that can waste their precious time and devastate dreams and aspirations. To stay away from these distractions, toppers have one strategy in place – Say No! They are well versed with the idea of saying 'No'. Toppers know how to stay away from distractions. However, this doesn't mean they don't indulge in fun. They do allot time for recreation and light exercises to stay fresh. These students always have their eyes on goal and accomplish tasks on time.

Combined Study

This is quite common among students. The process involves studying in group at a common place. Unfortunately, this process is exploited by most students in a negative way. They consider this an opportunity to sit together, gossip, and indulge in junk food. To utilise this time, one must focus on studies and getting problems solved.

Reaping the Benefits

In order to reap benefits of time management, one must learn what it is all about and the benefits it provides. Experts believe that time is a school which teaches some of the most important lessons of life. Students who waste time waste their life because nobody has ever been able to recycle it.

Time Once Lost is Lost Forever

Students know that time is precious and must be utilised to its fullest. However, there are only a few who actually follow this philosophy. This is also the reason that there are only a few toppers in educational institutions. If you wish to become a topper then it is crucial to realise the importance of time. Money once lost can be earned back. Deteriorated health can be nursed back. Lost properties can be bought back. However, time once lost cannot be earned, bought, usurped, or requested back.

Auspicious Time

Students have a tendency to wait for an auspicious time to kick start studies. However, no time is auspicious to start studies. It is all about starting off with the course curriculum and continuing with it. Waiting for the right time may leave you with no time in hand at all.

Pleasing Friends

Many students waste their time in pleasing friends. However, this is simply wastage of time. One needs to keep away from these activities to reach on top. Those who realise the importance of these facts and manage their time well can reach on the top.

Nothing is Instant

Nothing in this world is instant other than noodles. To be successful in life, one needs to schedule a timetable. Hundreds of students prepare for exams but only a few become topper. Toppers are usually students who schedule a timetable for themselves and follow it religiously.

Home Atmosphere

Students are more disturbed by the atmosphere at home than the exams. Parents and other family members create a very difficult environment at home during exams. They keep on reminding the student how tough things are going to be. Expectations and anticipations also tend to make students fear examinations. Hence, it is crucial to keep the atmosphere at home as pleasant and relaxed as possible.

Mismanagement of Time

Students are also afraid of mismanagement of time. They ignore the importance of time management during the start of session and tend to regret when it gets too late. They are unable to learn and revise lessons on time. Parents must support their children and help them realise the importance of time management.

Towards the end, we would like to emphasise on the importance of time again. Saving time is important in order to ensure its maximum usage. Time is a school that teaches many new and unique lessons. Using time constructively will help you become a topper.

Time is money. It should be treated with respect and used the best way possible. Hard work is very important to achieve success. However, it is equally important to value each second and use it wisely.

Here are some tips you must follow in order to understand the importance of time.

Top Tips

- Peaceful environment at home is crucial for better concentration on studies.
- Fulfilling dreams and desires is possible with a stress-free mind.

- Studying smart is the key to success. It is better than studying whole day and night without planning and strategies.
- Success isn't the key to happiness. It is happiness that leads to success. Studying lessons with love and complete dedication will help you do well in exams.
- Self-motivation is the best source of motivation for students.
- To bring out the best in oneself, one must get inspired by their own self.

11

Keeping Anxiety at Bay

The present age students are lucky. They have access to huge number of facilities and advanced technology. Right from laptops to computers, tablets, internet, and smartphones, students have everything that is needed to reach the top. However, despite so much to take help from, students remain anxious and live in stress all the time.

So what is the reason behind this constant worry? Why are students anxious all the time? What do they exactly want? What is their goal? Some students fear loneliness while others get anxious when surrounded by crowd. Examinations are the major concern among most students.

Problems are a part of life. Each one of us must deal with it at some point of time. For students, life has many challenges and fears. Fear of failure is one among them. Most students fear scoring less in exams while others fear remarks from parents and friends.

Did you know fear of 'what others will say' is the biggest illness a human being can deal with? The pressure of doing well in exams and scoring well among students often results in anxiety and stress. This also results in confusion and students are unable to prepare for exams. Negative way of thinking is also the main cause of fear faced by thousands of students across the globe.

One of the most common problems faced by students these days is their inability to concentrate inside a classroom. Some students are physically present in the class but their mind wanders elsewhere. Human mind has a tendency to think about mistakes in the past or dream about future prospects. So when the professor gives lectures, it never travels into the brain from ears. It simply bounces back into the classroom owing to the student's lack of focus on what is being taught.

There are many things that lead to anxiety in students. These include lack of nutrition, inadequate sleep, and choosing wrong time and method of study. You must have observed that many times, people say, something, feel something else, and do something entirely different. The confusion stops them from striking a balance between actions and thoughts. And those who try to balance the two are sometimes forced to follow what their elders guide them to. If you are serious about achieving success in life, then you must avoid getting distracted and focus on studying hard. This will open opportunities to become a topper.

There are times when students feel that they cannot concentrate despite revising a topic many times together. They also get disheartened due to this inability to concentrate. If a student is unable to focus or spends hours in chatting with friends, he is cheating on himself. Parents and teachers always advise students to focus only on studies. If entertainment is in mind, it is simply impossible to focus. Now the question is how to develop concentration? What is the key to focus on studies without getting distracted?

Schools students are like blank paper. Hence, parents and teachers should try to inculcate special quality and skills in them. These skills will help them build a secure, successful career in future. Now coming back to the point of concentration, it is important to focus on studies and everything taught by the teacher.

Staying awake late at night is not good for concentration. It also affects one's memory power. So it is always better to wake up early in the morning to study. This is the time when your mind is fresh and environment around is peaceful. It helps in building concentration and commit to memory whatever you learn.

Unfortunately, most students do not agree on this. They feel that if a lot of other things can be done during the day, it is possible to concentrate on studies as well. If you are not an early bird, make sure you find a peaceful corner in your house to study.

Taking small breaks between studies is important to relax mind and body and help it work better. So you can speak to a friend, take a stroll, or play a game to refresh yourself and recharge the body to work harder.

When learning something new or acquiring knowledge about a specific topic, it is important to keep your mind at peace. It should be free of stress and tensions. Studying in a calm and peaceful environment is the best way to memorise and understand the topics in detail.

Once, a student asked, "What should we do to get maximum marks in exams?" The expert answered, "You must learn to maintain a balanced state of mind."

So what should be done to keep mind in harmony? The best thing to do is avoid thinking about past or build castles in the air. Living in the present and trying hard is very important. To add some more weight to your learning, keep your mind cool, speech humble, and ears and eyes open.

The biggest problem faced by students of today is that they hate studies. They find it pretty boring and tiring. Well, thoughts of pessimism can make anyone realise that he or she is worthless. It is all in one's thought. If you think you can't, you simply will not.

Anxiety kills one's appetite. Students either start eating less or indulge in excessive binging. It also leads to physical weakness and mental fatigue among students which affects their studies. They face problems with studies and remain unsuccessful to cope with increasing pressure with time. The only solution to this problem is to fight off this feeling of negativity and stay away from stress as far as possible. Students must make efforts towards coming out of this situation before things get worse. Seeking support from parents, friends, and teachers will also help.

Toppers believe that one must develop a passion within to score high in exams. Lack of passion, urgency, enthusiasm, and ardour can be obstacles in the path of success.

Success can be achieved by preparing to face all kinds of challenges. This is possible when you work hard to compete with others. Unless you develop a keen desire to move ahead and reach the sky, it is not possible to become a topper.

Light exercises such as walking or cycling can help students keep stress and anxiety at bay. Also grab an opportunity to laugh or listen to music. These activities are mood enhancers. The more you stay away from anxiety, the better it gets.

Toppers from the past believe that it isn't necessary to stay glued to books 24 x 7. The key to success is knowing what to study and how. Regardless of the type of exam you plan to give, it is possible to achieve success in it. All you need to do is focus on studies without distracting yourself much.

Here are some tips given by toppers to helps students enhance their concentration power.

Top Tips

- Stress free environment is a must to concentrate on study.
- To fulfil dreams and aspirations, one must learn the art of keeping mind free of anxiety and stress.
- Adopt smart ways to study instead of the traditional method of spending hours together at the table.
- Success is not the key to happiness. Instead, happiness is the key to success. Hence, it is important to maintain peace while studying for exams.
- Self motivation is the biggest source of motivation.
- To perform your best, you must get inspiration from within.

12

Self Confidence

Battles are fought with weapons but won only through confidence. Here's is an example to help you know about the significance of self confidence. Once, a group of ten boys were asked to propose a girl. Eight of them brought red roses and expressed their desire. The ninth boy came with a ring. He was confident and knew that the girl would accept his proposal. Now you must be thinking what happened to the tenth boy? Well he came with his family dressed in a wedding suit. What would you call this attitude? This was over confidence.

Students must understand that there is a thin line difference between confidence and over confidence which should be realised and followed. Confidence is a very powerful tool. It helps a student fight all kinds of adverse situations.

Most students feel that they are equipped with adequate knowledge. But this is not true. There is no limit to gaining knowledge. The more you have the better it is! Confidence helps a student achieve the desired goal. It opens several new doors of opportunities.

There are many students who don't know the reason behind failure despite repeated trials and hard work. The only reason is lack of confidence which fills one with negative thoughts. This also restricts one from exploiting their full potential. Without confidence, one cannot accept new challenges. Fear of failure and criticism stops one from doing so. Hence, it is crucial to develop will power and confidence to take newer risks and challenges. Confident students take criticism in their stride and consider it as an opportunity to improve.

Self confidence is the most powerful weapon for a student. It helps them make efforts towards fulfilling dreams and aspirations. It gives birth to positive thoughts and gives enough courage to fight off all kinds of obstacles. However, make sure you understand the difference between self confidence and over confidence. Self confidence leads to success whereas over confidence is a sure shot path to devastation. So whether you are attempting pre-board exams or the finals, prepare well and stay equipped with all necessary information.

There are times when situations are not in our favour. Here, it is important to keep calm and avoid losing control over emotions. With patience, will power, and confidence, it is possible to win over the toughest of situations in life.

If you think you can win, the world is yours. On the contrary, if you feel and act like a loser, nothing can help you. So make sure you are always smiling and confident. Work hard and prepare well for exams. When it is time to give exams, simply stop thinking much about your problems and act. Relax and revise all that you have learnt and attempt the exams confidently.

A desire to climb the Everest is one thing and actually undertaking the task is entirely a different game. One needs to nurture courage and willpower enough to be able to accomplish big tasks and achieve bigger goals. Just as a single matchstick holds enough power to burn down the entire jungle, a spark of self confidence within you can help you do achieve all that you want. Hard work can change one's destiny for better. Students who don't do well in exams or are unable to achieve a desired goal lack self-confidence. The major difference between a successful and an unsuccessful student is the ability to make dream come true. The unsuccessful student dreams of becoming a topper whereas a successful student spends most of his time making dedicated efforts towards it.

It does not matter which section of the society a student belong to. To be a topper, one must have a strong will power and self confidence that does not waver at the harshest of situations faced. Those aspiring to become a topper do not worry about problems or criticism. Knowledge is the power they depend on. These students simply focus on doing something better than others.

We believe that this chapter has filled you with enough self confidence to help you achieve all that you want. Your determination and dedication towards becoming a topper will definitely help you become one. Once you have developed this feeling within you, nobody and nothing in this world can stop you from becoming a topper.

Top Tips

- If you nurture a strong passion within to become a topper, nothing can stop you.
- Excuses are used by those who lack self confidence.

- Stay away from negative emotions such as despair, dejection, depression, anxiety etc. and join hands with happiness, hope, confidence, and determination.
- Hopelessness leads to rejection. Hence, it is important to avoid this feeling to creep into your mind.
- The best time is today. Get up and start working!
- Ask questions and express doubts humbly to receive an answer not revulsion.

13

Solution to All Problems

Does it sound a bit strange? Of course, you must be thinking how is it really possible for a single chapter of any book to provide solution to all problems? Had it been true, then everyone in school would be a topper. No one would have worries. But you need to believe us. We are here to provide real solutions to all your problems.

When a teacher tried to explain this fact to a student, he said that it is definitely possible to have solutions to all problems until the problem is someone else's. The teacher tried to explain the student the present era is about problems and no one is without troubles. If we talk about students, those who remain unsuccessful in attaining highest of scores are troubled. On the other hand, those who have tried and achieved success are burdened with expectations from teachers and parents. Problem is all around us.

Some of the toppers who have achieved 100% marks in exams are unhappy because they need to work hard to maintain this position. There are students who are surrounded by suicidal thoughts just because they scored 99% marks – less than what they had expected. On the other hand, teachers are worried about completing the course on time while the principal wants to maintain record of good results in his school.

This is surprising but true that each problem has a solution. All one needs to do is know the root cause of problem and solve it. Just as your brain discovers a question and has an answer for it, finding solutions to a problem isn't rocket science.

In order to find a solution to a problem, simply try to adopt all various theories that you had learnt in the past. Just as a key is designed before a lock, each problem has a solution. In case of an adverse situation, give way to positive thoughts and stand right in front of a mirror. The person in the mirror will give you the solution.

So what is the secret of finding a solution? Just as every riddle has an answer to it, there is a solution to your problem regardless of how complex it is. Going back to the example of riddle, some may know the answer while others don't. Now this doesn't mean the riddle cannot be solved at all. Take a look at the staircase. The same staircase takes you up and also down. It depends on how you see it. Often solution is right behind us and we keep on searching for it in the front.

Reading this chapter will help you find solutions to your problems. It will also help you become a topper. All you need to do is believe in the fact that the mind which has given birth to a problem or doubt also has a solution for it.

Sometimes, it is good to take help from friends and family. When two minds work together, solutions come out fast. You will also feel relieved to have somebody to support you in the times of trouble. However, when discussing about a specific problem, it is important to avoid straying away from the subject. Straying leads to waste of time and energy.

Jealousy and ego are your biggest enemies. You must stay away from these to focus on becoming a topper. These negative emotions tend to drain all your energy and things may go against your expectations.

Being a topper is not a matter of destiny. It all depends on the efforts you make towards achieving your goal. Students label their lessons as easy and difficult. Whatever is easier to cram becomes their favourite and others are categorised as difficult. However, this is just a notion. Some students consider science as a difficult subject while others find the same subject easy. It is just in the mind. Since you don't have interest in a specific subject, you find it difficult.

Students also discuss about possible and impossible things in their life. However, impossible is nothing but a blockage in mind that doesn't allow one to try a specific task. This gives birth to negative emotions and a feeling that the task cannot be undertaken and accomplished.

Success depends on one's perspective towards life. Some students feel that examinations are the darkest period of their life. There is no light around. On the other hand, there are students who feel just the opposite. They only see one night arriving between two bright days.

Once you decide to become a topper, it is important to know what your destination is, where you stand at present, what is it that you are looking for, how much time it will take to reach the destination, what kind of obstacles you may face etc? You need to find answers to these questions in order to obtain your desired goal.

Friends are important in life. They show you the right direction and help you in the journey of success. Make sure you help your friends in studies, especially those who are weak. Helping others and spreading knowledge will help you boost your knowledge about various subjects.

Exams are an important part of a student. One cannot ignore it. There is no other way to assess a student's skill and abilities without tests and exams. However, students are still afraid of it and tend to get nervous each time they have to face it. Since there is no way you can avoid it, gather some courage, boost up your confidence, prepare well, and attempt it happily.

There are many students who don't study the whole year and show all of their passion and skills during the last three months of the session. This is the biggest blunder they make. To become a topper, you need to show the same passion and ardour right from the first day of your session.

It is important to understand that there is no shortcut to success. Once, a mother took her son to a Baba.

"My Son works very hard but he still fails in exams while all of his friends always manage to pass. Please do something Baba," the mother said.

"Take this black thread and tie on his wrist on a Saturday," the baba said.

"Will my son pass?" the mother asked.

The Baba smiled and said, "His friends will fail this time."

So instead of finding shortcuts, it is important to work hard from the beginning and focus on studies. This is the only way to get to the top.

Knowing about your innate skills is very important. Speak to your seniors, parents, friends, and teachers to know what qualities can help you achieve success in future.

Each student is bound to make mistakes. This leads to a lot of problems and miseries. However, instead of worrying about these problems, one must try and find a solution to it. The solution to every problem is within you. Also try not to repeat the same mistake again and again.

Here's how toppers try to solve their problems.

Top Tips

- Destiny favours the brave.
- Success is the combination of hard work and luck.
- Willpower, determination, and dedication in a person will definitely make one a topper.
- Waiting for the right time to study will never bring you success.
- No student is weak enough to be unable to set a big goal.
- One who thinks he had failed will definitely fail whereas a winner at heart can conquer the world.

14

Revolutionary Thinking is the Key

The students of modern age are advanced. Their appearance, actions, and everything they do is new, fresh, and unique. So what is the basic difference between students of modern age and their counterparts from the past? Most people feel that the major difference is in the way they think and react. Let's understand this with an example – a man belonging to Hindu religion gets converted into a Muslim by the evening. Nobody around noticed any major difference in his limbs, hair, eye colour, or facial features. The only difference was in his thinking. His thoughts transported him from one religion to the other.

The new generation feels that change has been in terms of financial situation, lifestyles, way of dressing, and perspectives towards various situations in life. This is what they feel is the real change. They also feel that change in one's thinking and way of accomplishing various tasks has brought about a revolution in the society.

Another interesting yet amusing change is the usage of words to represent various things and situations around. For instance, youngsters believe in using a lot of slang and short terms for various words. Connaught Place, a famous tourist place in Delhi is now referred to as C. P., pictures are referred to as pic, etc. In short, the newness of present generation has brought many twists and turns in the language used by youngsters.

The World Wide Web is the hub for students, these days. They prefer obtaining information on the internet instead of reading books. According to them, popularity of a specific style of book forces various other authors to imitate it. Of course, it would be quite boring to spend time reading books of same style. The internet is the most preferred medium as it provides new and most updated information on a number of topics as per the choice of user. Students are also bored of following the study pattern used by their ancestors.

It is true that the study pattern in olden days was boring. For years, teachers used one pattern to teach different subjects to students. Limited information was provided to students. Question papers were prepared in the same pattern with only a few questions twisted and turned to confuse students.

This pattern can be dangerous for modern age students who are looking forward to become toppers. This is the age of revolution and each student must learn something new, get new source of motivation, and most importantly, newer patterns of education in schools and colleges.

According to the new age thinking, it is important for students to face new challenges and learn new things each day. This is how they can realise their true potential and develop new skills. Most of the intelligent students get bored if they aren't exposed to new challenges or taught something revolutionary. To inspire students do their best, it is the duty of educational institutions to keep serving them with something new and unique on a regular basis.

Modern age is all about new gadgets, computers, internets, and laptops. These advanced gadgets and machines are an important part of a student's life. It helps them do something creative and gain more knowledge on different subjects.

According to experts, studying through books is different from studying with images. The latter method has more influence on a student's life. This is also the reason new age teaching techniques are different. Teachers prefer showing models and pictures to students to help them understand better.

A lot of students want to know about the style of preparation they must adopt during examinations to be able to score highest scores. Although many of our friends know the answer of this question, we would still like to repeat a few tips here. Some important preparations should be started a day before the examination. Don't ignore the importancc of sleep. It will help you relax. Also avoid attending exam on an empty stomach. This will keep you distracted due to hunger. Read the question paper completely. In case, you find a few of the questions complicated, don't worry. Simply try to solve the paper. Once you start, your memory will get refreshed. Make sure you give more time to question that carry more marks and less time to those carrying less marks. This way, you can complete the entire paper within the allotted time period.

Similarly, regular practise is the key to obtain mastery over various tasks. For instance, you must have seen the artists performing in circus. They practise day and night to be able to display unique and spine chilling talents. Anyone can gain expertise in their respective fields via practising daily. Students can also do the same.

Despite knowing everything that is mentioned above, some students like to go with the flow. They avoid attempting something new and challenging in their life. Starting off with something new and revolutionary is a hard nut to crack. One may face a lot of challenges and troubles while doing so. However, it is only those who dare to experiment get winning positions in the society. Their names are inscribed with golden words in history. Students who stand first in their respective classes are well aware that no subject is too easy to be conquered and too difficult to be beaten at. It all depends on how one takes these subjects and gain expertise over it.

Many students consider education as a burden. However, toppers know that studies can become a source of happiness in future. It is a challenge that helps each individual win the battle of life. Those who consider education as a source of burden and misery must realise the difference between misery and challenge. Misery leads a person to a state of depression whereas challenge makes a person strong and helps him emerge as a winner in the long run.

Making plans is important but no one can achieve success without executing these plans and working hard. The bigger the goal of life is, the more difficult it gets to achieve. Only hard work and dedication can make it possible for a student to reach the top.

Having a close look at the results in the past few years, it has been revealed that only those who have studied each course book with complete dedication were successful in attaining top positions. Toppers believe that moving in the right direction towards achievement of goal and focussing on studying course books can give desired results.

Top Tips

- Brain power increases with regular practise. Sitting idle is dangerous.
- Regular trials and efforts leads to long term success.
- Make code words and key words for every important topic. This will help you memorise them with ease.
- Understanding each subject well and doing better than the others will help you become a topper.
- Hundreds of students are aspiring to become a topper. You need to work really hard to get to the top.
- Living in the present is prudence. According to students who top, successful present automatically results in a successful future.

15

Haste Makes Waste

Troubles are an integral part of student life. However, these should never be a source of dejection. The key is to fight off these evils and focus on the aim of life. Unfortunately, lack of confidence makes students lose heart and give up without trying. In fact, most students depend on others to get their problems solved.

Some of the most common problems faced by students these days include lack of time, regular exams, inability to finish off course books within the required time frame etc. However, getting anxious and choosing the path of hastiness can make the situation worse. One must beat the stress by exercising patience. Patience is a virtue. It is precisely the state of endurance under difficult circumstances, which can mean persevering in the face of delay or provocation without acting on annoyance / anger in a negative way; or exhibiting forbearance when under strain, especially when faced with difficulties. Patience is the level of endurance one can take before negativity.

Students who exercise patience are usually the most successful. Self control and self confidence are other two most important elements that make a student climb the ladder of success. Believing in one's capabilities and bowing down in gratitude is the road to peace and best way to keep haste at bay. On the other hand, working hard and respecting time is an open invitation to success.

What is the haste for? Why is most part of a student life spent in haste? One of the major reasons is lack of organisation and effective execution of planning. Most students set their alarm clock every night but only to press the snooze button the following day. They love to sleep for another 5 minutes that turn into half an hour. Result – The day starts in haste and ends in haste.

A good day or a bad day – the decision depends on the student; how he starts and ends it. One wrong start can give birth to thousands of negative emotions within. However, leaving the bed 10 minutes earlier than usual can make all the difference. The entire day will be organised. The act lets students attend coaching classes on time and finish off the homework on time. It is always good to work hard and spend good number of hours to study. However, it is equally important to go on according to a time-table. Scheduling hours smartly will help you succeed in every phase of student life.

Each day opens up doors for new opportunities to do something new and creative. Some students belong to a category of 'brilliant learners but poor writers'. They don't focus on writing their lessons and practising well. Hence, they face problems while giving exams within a restricted time period. A classic example of inability to write appropriately is a simple sentence – "For all intensive purposes" which is written as "For all intents and purposes" by poor writers. There is a difference between the two phrases which forces the examiner to restrict the number of marks awarded to students.

It is important to focus on style and art of writing to be able to represent a specific topic the best way. A small error in writing can lead to blunders and irreparable losses. Here, I would like to quote an example of Hindi writing which created a lot of misunderstanding –

Once, the government announced 'Bandh' all over India. The government official asked his subordinate to spread the message – "Kal Bharat ko Band Rakha Jayega" (India will observe a Bandh tomorrow). Unfortunately, the subordinate who was appointed to make the announcement wrote "Kal Bharat ko Bandar Kha Jayega" (a monkey will eat up the country tomorrow). This may sound hilarious but the damage is irreparable!

Daily practise can help students resolve this problem. Writing helps learn and memorise better as compared to reciting a lesson orally. Reading and examining what has been written by you will help in realising the mistakes and then rectifying them in future. Although it is not easy to accept mistakes, success comes to those who do and rectify their mistakes on time.

'To win some you lose some' – This is not just an adage. This is a philosophy that should be followed by students to stay ahead of the competition. Unfortunately, not many realise this. To highlight the significance of this philosophy, I would like to quote an incident of student who used to spend most of his time studying (more than other students of his class) but never tried to organise and plan schedules smartly. Here's how he suffered –

Once while giving exams, the examiner asked this student – "What's the matter? Why are you so lost? Have you forgotten something?"

"Sir…I haven't forgotten anything….actually I prepared for tomorrow's test by mistake" the student replied.

The examiner tried to help the student.

"Don't worry my child. You simply write whatever you know," the examiner said.

The student decided to attempt the exam but realised that he had forgotten to bring pen.

"Take this pen. It works well!" the examiner said.

The student said, "Sir! I want a pen that writes well."

The examiner was shocked to hear this.

"My dear child! I wish you had utilised your precious time in studying well and in an organised manner than wasting it in such dim-witted acts," he said.

The students of fast paced world look for shortcuts for everything. Often they want their teachers to suggest some special ways that may help them reach to the top without wasting much time and efforts. Students who focus on learning new things and exploiting each opportunity that comes their way are known to be brighter than their counterparts. However, the key is to work in a disciplined manner under expert guidance to avoid losing presence of mind in haste.

Toppers never take their lessons for granted. None of the lessons are easy for them. Others are often on the hoof and make mistakes. They don't focus on important portions of a lesson and lag behind their counterparts. For question comprising of 20 marks, students are supposed to solve it via elucidating in few lines. This becomes really difficult for those who haven't prepared well. No wonder some of the students are awarded with about 80-90% marks whereas have to do with 50%.

For such students I would like to mention that although it is my duty to provide expert guidance and lead them to path of success, the journey is all theirs to cover. One must be armed with the best and complete information to ensure a safe and victorious journey to success.

Assessing the route map is crucial before starting off with a journey. This helps one know about risks they may face during their expedition. Knowing the risks involved and constructing a foolproof plan to deal with them will help one to achieve their goal.

Most of the toppers like to keep it simple but there are some techniques they adopt to achieve success. Here are some of the rules they follow:

Top Tips

- Being in haste creates a dangerous situation for students. It often forces them to act, speak, and think in different directions (they are always in a state of confusion).
- Most students waste their time thinking about future instead of focussing on how to make the most of present and its impact in future.
- One must be careful while attending exams. Rushing into solving queries can lead to inane errors.
- Improving handwriting is an important part of preparing for exams. This can help gain extra marks.
- Always keep a track of language used while attempting a theory test.
- Never lose hope!

16

Staying Ahead of Others

Students have friends whom they love and care for. However, when it comes to achieving goals and ambitions, each student wants to gain an edge over the other. The credit goes to the 'cut-throat' competition in today's world. Being on the top is a unique feeling. It attracts attention of teachers and fellow students who suddenly start considering toppers as hero figures and idolising them. Life is a race for students wherein they must catch speed in order to win.

Gathering praise has become more important for students than appreciating others. Kudos to the neck to neck competition and the spirit to stay a step ahead among students of present world! Competition is tough because the only a few (one or two) students are crowned as toppers towards the end of session.

When it comes to comforts and amenities, modern world students are equipped with all that is necessary to stay ahead. Parents make all efforts and spend significant amount of money to help their children achieve success in their respective fields.

With so much available to all, how is it actually possible to reach on top? What is it that can distinguish you from those who are well equipped like you and trying as hard? Well, staying ahead of curve is no rocket science. You need not go through scriptures and spend time cramming up a vast set of rules. There are some simple tips you must follow for the same.

Be a Tough Child

Do you remember your childhood? Well, all of us. After all, how can one forget such a beautiful phase of life? As children, we were naughty and loved to play pranks on other. One of the major traits of children is their stubbornness. A child will rave and rant for a toy until he gets it. In a way, the child holds remarkable talent to force his parents give him what he wants. This is what a student must develop. Persistence for achieving a specific goal is the key to success. So if you have been a tough child for your parents, it is time to exploit this talent to the fullest.

The Formula

Staying ahead of the curve simply refers to your position on the statistical bell curve, where the top of the curve represents the median, average result. Being ahead of the curve will help you represent the top percentile of results through some advanced skills or understanding that sets you apart. In short, you must do two things to stay on top:

- Do better than others
- Do things differently

This simple formula will help you win the race.

Planning is Important

When it comes to staying ahead of competition, almost all students nurture a burning desire for the same. However, none of them will have a foolproof plan or special understanding of achieving this goal.

Hard Work always Pays

Vigour and spunk are two valuable characteristics that can help a student achieve his goal. Every student is rich in these traits yet only a few exploit them to the fullest. To stay ahead of competition, one must work harder than their counterparts.

Knowledge is Power

We conducted a research on students who were declared as toppers consistently and tried to know the secret formula they followed. Most of the students agreed that the school type and capability of teachers don't matter much. All it takes to achieve success is to work harder and develop deep understanding of a specific subject. It is crucial to be acquainted with minute details of a subject and avoid skipping classes. Best students attend classes regularly and pay heed to lessons taught. Gaining knowledge about a specific subject in depth will help you solve complex queries in exams.

Reading vs. Writing

Each student has his own style of learning lessons and preparing for exams. Some are happier learning lessons from their course books while others like to prepare notes. According to a study conducted on some of the effective techniques of learning, writing notes have been considered the best. One can learn more effectively by writing than reading. The act of writing helps you clarify your thoughts, remember things better, and reach your goals more surely.

Know your Course

Deep acquaintance about course curriculum plays a pivotal role in staying ahead of the curve. Ignoring important topics and negligence in this matter can lead to severe damage.

Optimism is the Key

Embracing optimism is a must for all students. Just as a match stick is capable of burning down hundreds of trees, one negative thought can annihilate your chances of getting to the top.

Destiny is What You Make of It

There are times when a close friend or acquaintance emerges as a topper in the class. Most students have one way to deal with the situation – blame it on their fortune! Yes, a lot of students are seen cribbing on their bad luck and envying fate of their fellow students once the results are out. Is it the right approach? Certainly not! Luck definitely plays a part in one's life but it isn't as powerful as one's hard work, will power to win, and unwavering hope to reach at the top. The term LUCK can be elaborated as 'Labour Under Correct Knowledge'. So it is you who make or break your fate. The toppers know this and always work hard towards achieving their goals.

Countenance Matters!

Toppers always focus on their teacher's facial expressions while solving a query. This is also referred to as 'visual learning style' wherein a student understands better by looking at the teacher's face intently while he is teaching. Visual learners often prefer to sit in the front of the class and "watch" the lecture closely. This technique has stemmed from the theory that one understands and remembers things by sight. Students who look at teacher's face while learning can picture what is being told in their head, and they learn best by using methods that are primarily visual. They prefer to see what they are learning.

Auditory Learning Style

This is yet another very effective way of learning. Students who pay attention on verbal instructions given by the teacher in class and solving problems by talking about them are more successful than their counterparts. Many toppers are also seen using rhythm and sound as memory aids.

Quality over Quantity

Most students think that toppers are born at night. Those who study through the thickness of night always stand first in class! Well, this is just a myth. It is quality that matters not quantity. So, the style and technique you adopt while studying will take you to the top. Modern course curriculum comprises of complex subjects. Hence, one must adopt distinct and unique techniques to conquer the hassles they come across while learning lessons. Different subjects demand different treatment. For instance, subjects like Hindi, English, and History demand focus and repeated revision sessions. On the other hand, a student must adopt unique techniques to get a hold over other subjects like Science and Mathematics.

While studying mathematics, it is crucial to focus on solving huge number of sums for a single formula. This helps one learn new ways to solve different sums and fight off hassles while doing so. To sum up, there is no room left for making errors in exams.

Appreciate Criticism

Teachers are your well-wishers. As educators and mentors, they motivate, guide, and believe in you. They know about your capabilities and shortcomings. Hence, any criticism coming from them should be appreciated and accepted with gratitude. Unfortunately, the first reaction for most students is to defend themselves or worse yet to lash back. It is taken as a hurtful and demoralizing factor. In contrast, toppers view it in a positive way. They take it as their teacher's honesty and an opportunity for betterment. Hence, it is important to see if there's something you can change to make yourself better. And then make that change. Actually strive to do better and you'll end up being glad you made the extra effort.

Focus

Toppers love to focus on what they do instead of getting distracted to a number of other issues surrounding them. They follow the formula of 'doing one thing at a time'. The ability to focus is a secret element to success that often gets ignored. The more you can concentrate the better you'll do on anything, because whatever talent you have, you can't apply it if you are distracted. So if it is about learning to solve mathematical sums, take one sum at a time and focus on solving it till the end. Forget about everything else around you. 'Focus' is precisely what toppers do to achieve their goals.

Failure Precedes Success

Are you afraid of facing failures? All of us are! However, it is not wise to consider failure as the dead end of one's life. In fact, it is the stepping stone of success. When you fail at something, you are actually one step closer to finding a way that will succeed.

Most of the successful personalities across the globe have faced failures in life at first. Failure is an unwanted yet an important companion of success. Accepting, analyzing, dissecting, and looking at failure from every possible angle helps overcoming it. Without failure, there is no growth. Learn from mistakes will make you a topper.

Will Power

Strong will power is the most powerful tool for students. It helps them reach their goals and ensure success at every step. Students must hold on to their will power to get success in whatever they do.

Success Comes to those who Dare and Act

This is true. Success seldom goes to the timid or those who sit and hope without trying. It is the rarest gift of god and the hardest achievement of a man. Hence, it is extremely important to work hard to achieve your goals.

Burning Desire to Succeed

Toppers get inspiration from various sources in their life. They keep trying and treading on the path of success. Strong desire to succeed and achieving goals is what helps one reach their goals.

Today is a Gift

No wonder it is known as 'present'. Winning a race and staying ahead of competition always is possible only when students forget about the past and future and focus only on the present. Working hard in the present will make your future secure.

Please Yourself

A lot of students lag behind in an attempt to please their friends. They move out together, spend time partying, watching movies, and gossiping. This leads to nothing but waste of valuable time and money. Toppers don't do things to please others. They study hard and score well to please themselves. Successful students know that pleasing friends will not win scores in exams but winning scores can get them many friends.

We hope that the above mentioned tips will help you become a topper in your class.

Top Tips

- Listening is more important than speaking. Listening to mentors and teachers help you gain more knowledge.
- Pessimism can destroy bright future prospects. Hence, it is crucial for students to practise optimism.
- Accept challenges from others to emerge as a topper.
- Students who are expecting rich harvest in the form of being a topper must focus on sowing high quality seeds (hard work).
- Feel as a topper when attempting examinations to fill yourself with confidence.

17

Source of Inspiration

Once, a student tried to help his friend Aman.

"What's the matter Aman? Why are you looking so depressed?" he asked.

"My father.....He insulted me today!" Aman replied.

"Really? But how?"

"Today, he asked me if the brain and heart inside me are in working condition. I nodded in yes. Then he asked about kidney and liver."

The student was shocked at this. "Then what did you say?" he asked.

"I was quite surprised at my father's attitude this morning. So I told him that all of my body organs are functioning well and that is the reason I am standing in front of you," Aman replied.

"Then?"

"My father was in a bad mood. He shouted at me and said if all of my body organs are in working condition then why am I not working somewhere and earning for myself? Papa said that he would say three golden words for me which would bring some change in my life. I was happy at last thinking that he had something nice to say," Aman said.

"What did your father say?" The student asked.

"Do something worthwhile!" Aman replied.

"He called me a worthless creature," Aman added.

"So what next?" the student asked.

"I'm confused. It isn't that I don't want to study but there's no inspiration," said Aman.

"Your family is highly educated. Why don't you get some from them?" the student asked.

"Well, you're right. My mom is a teacher in school who earns around 20,000 rupees in a month. My father is a doctor whose monthly income is around 70-80,000 rupees. My paternal uncle is an engineer and works in a reputed firm. He's earning around 1 lakh rupees in a month. My grandfather is a government officer and earns 1.5 lakh rupees in a month. On the other hand, there lives a Dhongi Baba who earns many lakhs of rupees in a month. Now you tell me, where should I draw inspiration from?" Aman asked.

The student understood his friend's problem. He tried to explain, "Aman, it isn't possible to achieve goals without working hard towards it. The irony of life is that one always tries to achieve difficult or unachievable goals. In order to rise and shine, you must get out of this depressed state of mind. Fill yourself with some vigour and energy to be able to set and achieve targets."

"The best way to deal with problems related to exams is to develop a source of inspiration within. It should be strong enough to fill immense amount of strength and courage within to keep you going during tough situations. At the same time, you must choose a career for yourself and work towards achieving the goal," the student explained.

"This is the problem, my dear friend! I don't have a source of inspiration. Also I'm surprised at those who become toppers!" said Aman.

"Well, this is a common problem most students face at one point in life. Unfortunately, there's no magical instrument that can help you with it. None of the astrologers or tarot readers can tell you about a specific source of inspiration that can work for you. It is up to you entirely. One must develop enough will power to find inspirational sources around. Most importantly, you must realise that will power and skill are interrelated terms," the student elucidated his point further.

Aman wasn't fully convinced.

"Inspiration can be taken from anywhere. It is all around you. Nature is the biggest source of inspiration. For instance, you can learn a lot from a flowing river. It is always consistent and flowing despite facing a lot of hassles in its way such as heat from the sun, rocks, the desert, etc. However, nothing stops it from reaching its final destination – the Sea. Like a river, going with the flow will help you achieve success in life. The key is to keep going until you reach your final goal. The sea waves are a strong source of inspiration for students. Despite many falls, they don't stop and keep trying until the destination is reached."

"A student can get inspired from a soldier on duty at the border. He stands tall and sacrifices his life for us. Duty comes first for a true soldier. As students, we must put our duties (study) first. The idea is to set some priorities in life and work on them. It is all about spending a few years studying hard and reaping the benefits for the rest of life. Students aspiring to become toppers can take inspiration from anywhere. There are sources all around you. All you need to do is realise the importance of these sources."

Aman was quite surprised to hear his friend's words. "This sound strange as I have always heard that one must have a role model to get inspired from and whom they should follow."

"You're right, my friend. But these sources have ephemeral effect on us. For instance, if you get inspired by a famous leader today, you may forget his speech and work a few days later. Similarly, if you get inspired by a movie star, the feeling stays fresh until he's in news. The moment another actor makes his mark; the movie star goes out of sight. Sometimes, it is possible to consider a fellow student as a role model once he tops and so on. All of this happens because our mind is occupied with thousands of things at a time."

"Finding motivation within oneself is the best way to achieve success in life. Getting to know the intricacies of your own inspiration can have lasting effects. By accepting and acting upon the things that stimulate, one begins to understand what it means to work hard and achieve success. So compete with yourself. Try to be a better student than you were yesterday. Instead of searching for an icon, just say, 'I can'. Success is not about getting inspired from great personality but turning into one and inspire others. Pessimism leads you to destruction whereas optimism is the key to success."

Aman was developing keen interest in his friend's advice.

"Have you ever noticed the impact of negative thinking on health? A lot of people tend to fall sick and suffer from serious diseases simply because they are pessimists. I would like to explain this theory with an interesting story," the student said.

"Long time ago, there lived a group of frogs in a pond. One day, the frogs held a meeting to discuss about shortage of food in the pond. One of the frogs suggested a shift to the nearby mountain. According to the frog, the place was rich in food. However, his companions didn't agree to the suggestion. They believed that it wasn't possible for them to climb up a mountain so high. While the frogs were busy discussing, the frog climbed the mountain and had his food. He returned back and told that the place above the mountain was fabulous with a lot of delicious food to relish. His counterparts were surprised to hear this. Upon being asked how he climbed the mountain, he said, 'When you guys were discussing about your inability to climb the mountain, I closed my ears to keep your pessimistic thoughts away. I focussed on positive thoughts and climbed the mountain on my own' the frog replied."

"My friend, talking big will not give you success. Optimism is the ultimate survival skill for students. Optimism has been proven to improve the immune system, prevent chronic disease, and help people cope with unfortunate news. Aman, was it possible for our freedom fighters to throw the British out of country without believing in their capability to do so?" the student asked.

Here, a lot of students must be thinking that true inspiration can be drawn from a single person. But this is not true for students of modern world. Our parents are the best persons to suggest different ways to study. On the other hand, what to study and the number of hours to which topic deserves a specific number of hours is best explained by teachers and mentors. Studies conducted have revealed that successful students can get motivated by different people at different stages. The most influential element is optimism. It helps students stand toppers in their respective subjects.

Students who allow negative thoughts to develop within tend to get intimidated by the very thought of giving exams. Fear is devastating. It is sad but true that a lot of student suffer from suicidal thoughts due to fear of exams. Negative thoughts are known to be the trigger factor for suicidal thoughts among students. It is better to keep a distance from such students as negativity is infectious. They may influence into gearing exams.

A famous Hindi movie dialogue says – "Jo darr gaya wo mar gaya" (fear kills). Exams are no monsters to get intimidated by. With hard work, will power, and positive thinking can help you overcome all kinds of fear and succeed in exams.

The key to overcome this fear is to realise one's true potentials. Toppers believe in fighting off all kinds of fears that attack them during the process of preparing for or attempting exams. They don't get affected by hurdles (big or small) that come their way.

When preparing for exams, one shouldn't ignore minute details. Make sure you revise all that you have learnt through the day prior to hitting the sack. You need to think of the problems you've suffered from through the day, complex topics, and things you'd like to work on again.

Each day should start by assessing what you had learnt. In case, you face some difficulty in a specific subject or topic, try to solve it by yourself or speak to your mentor about it. Your study schedule should be similar to preparing a CD (Compact Disk). Whatever you record on it will serve as notes for your forthcoming exams. The clear and crisp notes on the CD will not only help you with exams but allows the examiner to check papers without facing much difficulty.

Experts in the field of education feel that there's nothing as 'impossible' and 'extremely tough' for students. Every problem has a solution provided you make dedicated efforts towards it. Successful students take studies seriously in their school, college, and every other institution they join. So how to take studies seriously?

It is not the length of life but depth of life! Swami Vivekananda had a short yet meaningful life. He made huge achievements that may be impossible for men to achieve in many hundreds of lives. Quality of life matters more than the quantity. Some people live short but extremely meaningful life as compared to others who live hundred years of meaningless life.

It is natural to get inspired by some great personalities we hear, read, and write about and in an attempt to be like them, we lose our identity. All of us fear negative things and try to avoid them as far as possible. We are under the notion that negative things in life can thwart success. Although this is true to a great extent, there are many instances where students have drawn inspiration from negative situations in life and found some amazing ways to emerge as winners.

Students who have reached from floor to sky i.e. toppers admit that they spend 5-10 minutes extra daily in their coaching classes. Sometimes, they have to face the wrath of their teachers and mentors for pestering them. However, these students don't let their teachers rest until the problem is solved.

Inspiration can be taken from a lot of things around us. However, students must focus on developing motivation as a habit. The best thing to do is get inspired from an obstinate child who knows how to get what he wants. Similarly, it is important to stay determined and work hard towards being a topper until you become one. One must have a keen desire to learn in order to enjoy the taste of success.

A lot of students say that they spend entire night studying but fail to win over the destiny. But this is far from truth. Hard work always pays. If you are working hard but have failed to achieve desired goals, then you have not been trying too hard.

Here, we would like to share an interesting story of three boys from a village who decided to become toppers. They chose a cool quite place to learn their lessons. One day, a teacher saw these boys busy in studies while he was crossing the river. The teacher asked the boatman – "Who are these boys? What are they doing here?"

The boatman narrated the tale of three boys and their determination.

"Can you take me to that place?" the teacher asked.

The boatman took the boat to the spot where the boys were revising their lessons. He talked to the boys and gave some important tips. He then sat on the boat and continued his journey. After a while, the teacher observed some strange sounds in the water. He turned back and was taken aback to see the three boys chasing him through water.

"What's the matter?" he asked.

"Sir! Can you please explain the tips again? We would like to memorise these again and ensure success in the exams," one of the boys said.

"But how did you manage to walk through the river?" the teacher asked.

"We don't know, Sir! We just wanted to know the tips and techniques from you," the students said.

"Well done, boys! Just as you crossed the river with dedication to achieve your goal, keep studying, and preparing for your exams. Let this dedication be your sole inspiration to reach the top," the teacher advised.

There is absolutely no need to look up to a role model or an icon to achieve success in exams. What really matters is one's dedication, hard work, and complete focus on goals. Many students want to know about the best way to study. This is quite similar to a situation where a person is offered a plate full of delicacies and he want to know how to finish it off. Well, this means that the recipient of food isn't really hungry. One who is hungry will simply start relishing the food without asking questions. Similarly, one who is seriously interested to emerge as a topper would simply start off with the lessons instead of wasting time asking how and what to do.

Students learn a lot from their teachers and from time. There's a difference between time and teacher. A teacher teaches a lesson and then takes an exam whereas time takes an exam and then teaches a lesson.

Listed below are some of the thoughts that inspire toppers.

Top Tips

- Advice from a teacher tastes bitter initially but spreads sweetness when adhered to.
- Once a topper, one works hard to reach other goals of life.
- It isn't possible to accomplish big and important tasks unless you think of them.
- Don't fear those who pass comments on you. It is always the audience that makes noise not the player.
- Brilliant students don't do things for themselves but they set examples for others.
- Toppers don't leave any opportunity to learn.

18

Self-Discipline

What is the connection between success and self-discipline? Well, before discussing this topic, it is crucial to understand the definition of self-discipline. The ability to control one's feelings and overcome one's weaknesses or ruling over one's feelings is referred to as self-discipline.

Now the question is 'what is the role of self-discipline in one's achievement of success?' Well, just as machine owner has a control system in place, self-discipline is the natural control system of life.

A student can benefit from exercising self-discipline in his life. They would need it at every phase of their life. The universe is governed by laws of discipline. Right from sun to star, clouds, and many others, each element of Nature follows certain rules and regulations. If you are looking forward to remove darkness and shine in the sky like sun, you must rise before the sun rises in the sky and study hard.

Students who follow self-discipline in life are more successful than their counterparts. They have everything well-organised. Without self-control, the life of student is like a kite without string. It flies around aimlessly. Self-discipline is all about following a set of rules. Just as Mother Nature follows certain rules and accomplishes various tasks within a specific time-limit, students must follow discipline to become toppers.

One of the rules a student must follow is to use a proper study table for learning lessons. Use of bed or sofa for studying leads to drowsiness and lethargy. A lot of students learn the lesson of self-discipline from their parents and develop it as a habit. This helps them achieve success in various spheres of life. In order to get a task right it is important to follow the path of discipline.

The significance of self-discipline can be observed in the army. Right from Jawans to Majors and Colonels, each employee of Indian army follows a set of rules to ensure safety for citizens of our country.

Now the question is how self-discipline is important for students. What role does it play in student life? Well, once, a teacher asked students to accomplish their task within a specific time period. He also asked the students to prepare a time table to finish off the task by building a time table.

However, the students revolted.

"Sir, we can finish off the course curriculum without using any time table," they said.

The teacher said, "In order to accomplish a task within a given time frame, it is important to prepare a time table."

One of the students said, "The railway division of India makes a time table every month but most of the trains fail to reach on time. So, what is the use of such a time table?"

Another student said, "My dear friend, the time table will help one know which train is late by how many hours!"

"I know it was a joke! But it still has a message which is loud and clear. Unless you make a time table, it isn't possible to know about your preparation for the exam," the teacher said.

"With a schedule in hand, you'll know about the topics that have been left untouched. Apart from schools, colleges, and exams, having a well planned time table is extremely helpful in daily life too. Maintaining discipline in day to day life will help in managing time and finishing off simple to complex tasks without much difficulty," the teacher explained.

Now that you know how important scheduling a time table is for adept preparation of exams, it time to kick start with the process. However, make sure that the time table is practical and easy to follow. Plan it in a way to have ample time for study and some room for household tasks. This will help you under situations wherein some urgent house work crops up and wastes your valuable time.

The time table should be prepared according to one's abilities and situations at home. Each student is different, has unique capacity to study, and lives in different conditions. Hence, it is important to schedule an agenda accordingly.

Some students try and do things that are far from their capacities. They decide to spend the entire night studying but are unable to keep up with the promise. Here, we are not discouraging a student's aspirations. We just want to help students prepare an agenda that is practical and easy to follow.

Lack of discipline can prove dangerous for a student especially when it is time to give exams. Success in exams depends on certain factors including one's level of interest in studies, commitment towards preparation of exams, etc. Each student holds some unique skills and limitations. It is about realising the potential within and making dedicated efforts towards the goal.

Whether it is about getting top marks in an exam or being a topper in a competition, one must realise and believe his true potential. Each goal has some specific demands which can be fulfilled only if the student makes dedicated efforts towards developing deep understanding of a topic, expertise in the subject, and fluency in language.

Discipline is important in the field of education. Right from paying heed to what teachers explain in the class to understanding the subject in detail, one must have full control over emotions, behaviour, and other traits. Listening to lectures is more important than speaking on a specific topic. Many times, students get benefited from simple tips and techniques offered by teachers and professors.

Here is an interesting incident to elaborate the importance of self discipline in a student's life:

Once, a teacher chided a student hard for not doing homework for days together. The student couldn't control his anger and retaliated, - "Don't you know how to deal with a customer?"

Well, it is true that teachers are paid for home tuitions and coaching classes. However, they are still our mentors and guide. They hold a special place in our life and it is our duty to respect them.

In ancient years, teachers were considered as 'Guru' and highly respected by students. Their instructions were followed by students without questions and complaints. Situations may have changed with advent of modern technology but a teacher is still our guide who directs us towards the path of success.

To acquire knowledge from a teacher, we must respect him and believe in him. You cannot receive knowledge without clearing your mind of malice. It isn't possible to add new things to a container without removing the contents inside. A jar filled with milk must be emptied and washed thoroughly prior to storing fresh milk. You cannot store new data on hard disk of a computer which is already overloaded with files.

The same theory is applicable to uncontrolled human brain. It isn't possible to store new information given by a teacher without refreshing the brain. A student must keep his brain open to be able to allow in some new interesting facts from the educator.

Many students expect their teachers to teach as per their own convenience. However, this is not practical. Each student must follow discipline and some rules to be able to emerge as a topper in school, college, and examinations. Education and discipline go hand in hand. Certain amount of self-control is crucial for every student to be able to reach a specific goal.

Being a topper is no child's play. One needs to toil extremely hard to be able to reach the zenith. According to a famous adage, travelling to a river isn't enough to quench thirst. One must bow down a little to be able to drink water. Similarly, a student must respect and believe in his teacher to be able to acquire the wealth of knowledge.

As already mentioned, discipline must be exercised in day to day life in order to be successful. Just as healthy diet is important to maintain a healthy body; one must get 7-8 hours of uninterrupted sleep daily to stay healthy and alert through the day. A good night's sleep can fill you up with energy. William

Shakespeare had referred sleep as the greatest nutrition for body and brain.

Student of modern age are fully aware of the significance of sound sleep and its impact on health. However, they ignore its importance and dig their faces into books whole night during exams. One needs to utilise time resourcefully to be able to study well for exams. Youngsters of today take time for granted. For instance, you must have heard students making plans for the next day. When scheduling a meeting, they would usually say, “I’ll be there in a day or two”. Now this can be confusing. The answer should be precise (one day or two days). There’s a gap of 24 hours within a day and the number of hours can make a huge difference in a student’s life.

Time is the most precious thing for a man as it comes only once in someone’s life and never stays long. Time management is basically planning and dividing one’s time in a constructive way. We all have a number of activities that have to be taken care of in a particular period of time. So we should be able to plan our activities in such a way that we are able to complete all the work in a given span of time.

Time once lost, can never come back. To illustrate my point, I would like to make a few comparisons: - To know the value of one year, ask the student who failed. Hence, it is crucial to schedule a time table and finish off important tasks as per the schedule. It isn’t wise to postpone today’s task for tomorrow as you never know what the other day has in store for you.

When you schedule a time table, make sure you work accordingly. No one (regardless of how wealthy he is) can buy time and use it as per convenience. Time is constant. None of the powerful emperors were able to rule over it. No scientist can control it with his inventions. You simply need to respect time and keep going with it.

Maintaining and following discipline is important all through the academic year. However, it becomes more important to follow it during exams. Luckily, technological advancements and advent of computer and World Wide Web has made it extremely easy for students to look for solutions on complex topics. However, one must exercise control while using internet. The technology must be used only for studies.

Some students are under a notion that writing more than required while solving a question paper will fetch them more marks. However, this is not true. Using fancy techniques to solve question papers and writing more than required will only spoil things. The idea is to keep it simple. Give straight, to the point answers to a question.

Exercising discipline is important while following a diet. However, the students of today don't follow it. They believe in having food whenever they want. Hence, late night snacking is very common among youngsters today. This is hazardous for health and tends to retard functioning of brain. Influence of western culture on youngsters is huge. This has given birth to immense love for junk food, tradition of late night snacking, partying etc. Keeping these habits at bay and focussing on studies is the only way to excel in exams.

There is a difference between buying toys made of clay and gold ornaments. The former can be acquired easily. On the other hand, one must work hard to possess the later. Similarly, it takes a lot of efforts to become a topper. It is about realising the importance of environment and fresh air before it is too late and you require roaming around with an oxygen mask.

You must have seen people making preparations ahead of time for a family outing or trip. However, they simply ignore the importance of scheduling a program for forthcoming exams. Apart from studying hard, one needs to keep working on enhancing personality. So when preparing for being a topper, you must exercise some self control and follow rules that take you to the top.

Here are some important things toppers have learnt from practicing self-discipline.

Top Tips

- Self-discipline is the stepping stone to self-development and success.
- One is never alone with significant goals to achieve in life.
- Money cannot buy courage. One must develop it within.
- Accomplishing a task effectively and successfully without the fear of being criticised is important.
- Self-discipline is best learnt by a student at home.

19

The Tale of Success

Becoming a topper is neither difficult nor impossible. In this chapter, we will discuss about how the tale of success is scripted. What are toppers really made of? What qualities distinguish them from others?

Most students are intimidated by the term, 'final exams'. 'Time flies', they think once they have the date sheet for final exams in hand. There are many students who don't focus on studying well the entire year and regret once the exams draw near. This is the time when they get serious and start reading and cramming up course books seriously.

Although this approach won't help you acquire a winning position in class, confidence and hope will help you become a topper. Each student dreams of scoring highest marks in the exams but only a few manage to attain this position. If you are determined to do so, here are some crucial points to keep in mind:

Self-Confidence

Being a topper is tough. After all, proving oneself and standing above hundreds and thousands of other students is no child's play.

So how do toppers survive? What do they do to reach to the top? Self-confidence is the key here. It motivates a student to work hard and keep progressing towards the goal. Students with high level of confidence usually achieve great heights of success.

Nurturing Desires

A human desire is born twice.

Once - When you dream of achieving something.

Second - When the dream is fulfilled.

Hence, it is important to keep nurturing the desire within until it gets fulfilled. You must think of the desire 24 x 7 and keep making efforts towards it. This is the difference between a topper and other students. Toppers dream of reaching to the top and don't rest until they reach their goal. The key is to allow your dream to enter and rest into your sub-conscious mind.

Clearer Dreams

Dreams can have a powerful effect on our waking lives. They reflect our hopes and fears about the future. What are your deepest dreams and desires? What do you really want? The fulfilment of a specific dream starts with intention and desire. Destiny is shaped by one's deepest intentions and desires. You are what your deepest desire is. Your dream is more likely to come true if you first see it clearly in your mind. It is crucial to develop a clear vision of what you want and be specific with your intentions. This will help the universe get a crystal clear structure to work with. There is an incident where a student once dreamt of having a huge fleet of cars around him that used to move and stop with his instructions. He definitely wanted to become a rich man. However, what he ultimately ended up becoming was a traffic policeman. This was the sad result of unclear vision of goals and desires. Hence, students must dream and desire clearly what they want.

Hope for the Best

Toppers have great hopes. They stay positive in all situations and work hard. So if you wish to become a topper, it is crucial to be hopeful and think positive always.

Blue Eyed Baby

Each year, thousands of students clear competitive exams. However, only a few become toppers. No wonder being one is such a tiring and extremely difficult task. Toppers are treated as heroes of the class, school, or college. Teachers and professors treat them as their blue eyed baby. They are as good as gold and respected by all. If gold must be gold, it must pass through fire. Similarly, a topper is run through stringent tests and examinations to turn into the most valuable being among the rest.

Goals are Important

Prior to scripting the tale of success, one must realise their goal in life. Setting goals is a fundamental component to long-term success. Knowing one's priorities and goals in life will help one attain success in every sphere of life. Most students study just for the heck of studying. They hate the very sight of books and even delay studies. If these are the situations that keep you occupied, becoming a topper is not your cup of tea. Toppers know their priorities, have clear goals in mind, and keep trying to achieve them until they are successful.

Life is what you make of it!

Here is an interesting incident to help you connect with the significance of this adage. Once, a mouse got into a train. The passengers saw the mouse. Soon the train was under a storm. Some of the passengers jumped with fear, some hid themselves into the corner of their respective berth while others kept an eye on the entire scene. They simply enjoyed the game. On the other hand, one of the passengers was unmoved by the incident. He kept on working on his laptop without moving his head to see what's happening around him. This passenger was a student who had his eyes set on a goal and his focus on finishing off a specific task. Toppers are the same. They are known to possess incredible concentration power. They also hold immense potential to stay glued to a set schedule until it is accomplished successfully. This is because toppers are passionate about studying and gaining knowledge. So they aren't aware of what's happening around them. The sound of television never reaches their ear. They are never disturbed by guests arriving or any other activities running around the house. All they are concerned about their studies and their goal – to become a Topper!

Hard work is the Only Truth

Wish to acquire topmost position in class, school, college, or an entrance exam? You must do whatever it takes to reach there. Depending on magic and miracles will only waste your precious time. Take the whole responsibility on your own shoulders, and know that you are the creators of your own destiny. Most successful personalities agree that one is responsible for what they are, and whatever one wishes themselves to be, they possess the power within to make themselves. So whatever you wish to be in future can be produced by your actions and thoughts in the present actions. The idea is to act and hope for the best.

The Power of Knowledge

There are two things that can help you become a topper – Knowledge and Education. So make sure you equip yourself with these powerful tools to achieve the desired goal. Each day should start and end with acquiring knowledge and complete focus on studies. Most of the toppers across the globe agree that success would have been impossible without proper knowledge and apt educational qualification.

Be Different

Modern students are well aware of the fact that it takes a lot of efforts and planning to accomplish an extraordinary task. To do something exceptional, one needs to get into unique planning and strategy building. Toppers aren't ordinary beings. They are different from other students. Hence, in order to reach above others, you must do what others don't. A little sacrifice at initial stages goes a long way. So make sure you avoid joining other students in unnecessary partying, laundering, and gossiping sessions. Dedicate yourself to studies to be able to emerge as a topper.

Optimism Works

At the beginning of session, most students are doubtful about scoring well in the finals. However, as the session begins and goes on, they start believing in their potential. Optimism within bright students helps them focus on studies and gain knowledge. Knowledge is power. This is a tool that helps each one of us move ahead in life and achieve desired goals.

Work Hard

Toppers aren't born out of miracles. They are hard workers and committed towards their goals. They usually start preparing for exams seriously to be a topper. This helps them achieve their goal without difficulty. Such students try and find out the best within themselves. Learning new things daily is extremely important for students to be able to gain knowledge that proves helpful in the long run.

Toppers don't Belong to a Class

It is a common notion among people that only students belonging to a specific category become toppers. They feel that only students belonging to elite class are capable of becoming a topper. The notion has been developed from state of the art schools these children get educated from and best of teachers visiting their homes to give tuitions and additional coaching.

However, this is not the truth anymore. A lot of students belonging to lower and upper middle class sections are fetching brilliant marks in exams. India also has many toppers from the poor section of society. It precisely depends on the student, his abilities, and determination to do something big in life.

To Win Some You Lose Some

While scripting this chapter of the book, we had an opportunity to meet a highly qualified professor.

"Sir, how is it really possible for any student to become a topper?" we asked.

"It's simple. Each student is given an opportunity to enjoy, have fun, and freedom to skip classes. Those who don't take advantage of this golden opportunity become toppers," the professor explained.

Direction is Better than Speed

Reaching to the top isn't difficult for students. Brilliant students know the significance of direction over speed. Most of the time, drivers are so busy looking at the speedometer that they forget about the milestone. As long as you have goals and are taking right steps towards them, it doesn't matter how long it takes to reach the destination. There will always be obstacles (big or small); there will always be some back-pedalling. However, you must think of these as opportunities to refocus. Walk down the wrong path can lead to a number of problems. Hence, it's always better to go backwards and start again, then to keep walking in the wrong direction. The right direction is usually shown by a teacher. Relying on your mentor will help you tread along the path of success.

Revise Well

Toppers from schools and colleges believe that going through a topic once or twice isn't enough to retain information until the exams finally arrive. Hence, they focus on revising a topic again and again to understand it in detail and commit to memory.

The 8 Golden Hours

A day comprises of 24 hours. Students spend 8 hours in school and travelling. Another 8 hours must be dedicated to sleep. Now, one is left with only 8 hours to accomplish Mission Topper. Students who utilise these 8 golden hours are usually the most successful ones.

It is your Success

Success is not determined by what others think of you or expectations others have from you. It is about your goals and expectations. Achievements and laurels are just a part of life. The essence is to work hard, learn new lessons, and whether or not you have been successful in achieving targets set by you.

Family Support

A student cannot reach new heights of success without the support of his family. Ample love and support from each family member will work as a pillar of strength for students. Parental support also serves as a source of inspiration for students. They feel like an earthen lamp that isn't afraid of darkness. It keeps spreading its light all around. There is dawn after every dark night.

Guidance from Mentors

Brilliant students are always in touch with their teachers. Problem solving plays an important role in student's life. Hence, it is important to take help of a mentor whenever you face a problem. It helps boost basic knowledge about a topic and get you acquainted with several new methods to solve a problem.

Aspire to Acquire

Nurturing a desire to be a topper and becoming a topper are two different things altogether. It is easy to aspire to be a topper than to be a topper actually. A lot of students fail due to lack of confidence and various other problems they face.

Secret Formula

We believe that each student holds adequate potential to be a topper. All it takes is realising one's true potential and make dedicated efforts. You must have enough faith in your capabilities and a burning desire to be a topper.

Once, a student asked us about the secret formula to become a topper. We simply asked him to forget about becoming a topper and focus on studying as hard as possible. "Your focus and dedication towards study will make you a topper," we explained.

A student must develop a keen desire and unwavering commitment towards becoming a topper, nothing can stop him.

Here are some effective strategies to help you succeed in your mission.

Top Tips

- Dedication, hard work, and focus can help any student become a topper.
- Destiny and luck lines are mere myths. A student with enthusiasm and zeal to become a topper will become one anyway.
- Problems and lack of amenities are not hurdles big enough to stop a student from becoming a topper. One simply needs to work hard and keep his eyes on goal to succeed.
- Toppers don't waste time chasing worthless things. They believe in their potential and exploit it to the fullest to achieve their goals.
- Toppers don't believe in wasting time with idle friends and classmates. They utilise their time in chasing mentors and educators to solve problems.
- Toppers don't regret about their mistakes in the past or waste time worrying about what future has in store for them. They make the most of present and the time they have in hand.

20

Topper's Top Tips

In this chapter of the book, we will again focus on all aspects of being a topper. Earlier, we have discussed crucial elements about the significance of education and preparation to emerge as a topper in detail. Students of the modern world have to face stiff competition at every phase of their life. Unfortunately, knowledge alone isn't enough to conquer this cut throat competition. No wonder a lot of teachers and parents put immense pressure on students. "This is the time – Do or Die" – they would say. However, this rule doesn't apply on optimistic individuals. Bidding adieu to life is the last thing they think about.

We strongly recommend students to utilise moments prior to exams. The focus should be on preparation. The time demands your complete dedication and commitment towards goals. So equip yourself with arms and set out for the battlefield with an aim to win.

Toppers don't win smaller games. They are made for bigger battles and challenges. Burning the midnight oil without backing it with sound strategies is not their cup of tea. According to psychologists, hard work alone cannot take one to the top. Unwavering determination to achieve something in life is what works. Thoughts have a huge impact on physical being, emotions, and brain. Apart from hard work, perfect control over one's emotions is crucial.

Detailed analysis of different traits of a student will help in revealing strategies and techniques that helped him emerge as a topper. According to a study conducted on some of the highly successful students, it was revealed that those who achieved immense success in their respective fields share similar capacities. Some of the major similarities shared by these students include endless enthusiasm to achieve a goal, optimistic approach to life, self-confidence, punctuality, and control over negative emotions.

Students who dream of achieving success have an optimistic approach towards life. They have one thing in their mind – to achieve goal and work towards it wholeheartedly. Building a structure and preparing for examinations hold a lot of similarities. The foundation needs to be stronger to support the building. Aspiring toppers should understand this.

The key to become a topper is to do things differently and stay ahead of thousands of other students preparing for the same. So what to do? How to act differently and what is it that one requires doing to stay ahead? Well, as a student, you must make dedicated efforts towards knowing the 'difference' between toppers and those who lag behind.

According to experts, half the battle is won the moment a student adopts optimism as the way of life. Optimism helps students keep anxiety at bay during exams. They are happy, confident, and hopeful which distinguishes them from other students.

God has made us all equal. Students are no exception. Although all students are not equal, each one of them has special quality that distinguishes them from others. Some students feel that they work very hard but remain unable to achieve deserved success. Is it true? Well, we believe that what these students say is far from truth. Dedicated students never fail to achieve their goals. It is all about the amount of efforts and percentage of dedication they put in.

Apart from working hard and preparing well, one needs to follow self-discipline, punctuality, and optimism. Most importantly, toppers are well aware of their strengths and shortcomings and their field of interest.

So before the final arrival of your exams, let's have a quick look on some valuable tips of becoming a topper:

Revolutionary Outlook

Although the techniques and methods mentioned in this book above have made your job easy, we believe that it is important to acquaint you with some unique qualities that will help you become a topper. Present era is marked by cut throat competition. Hence, it is crucial to discover new and advanced educational techniques to have an edge over your competition.

To emerge as a winner, you must develop traits which is absent in other students. The modern world has brought huge transition in techniques and methodology of carrying out varied tasks. Education is no different. Working at snail's pace may prove hazardous for students of today. The idea is to stay consistent in efforts and commitment towards learning new things. Just as every dark night ends with a brighter day, each moment in the life of a prospective topper should be filled with hope. Let despair and dejections end as the sun rises on a new day.

A lot of students simply focus on their curriculum. Thinking out of the box isn't a common culture among scholars, these days. This is also the reason most students lag behind. One must acquire ample knowledge about various happenings across the globe. Right from politics to movies, sports, science & technology, and research, students should be aware of everything around them.

In a formal interview conducted with toppers across India, most of them agreed that they did more than just cramming up their course books. They are more interested in knowing about new things in life and latest advancements. The more you learn, the more you gain!

Take Help – It is Important

Students have a peculiar habit of taking it lightly, once the course study is over. They feel as if they have cleared the examination. This is a dangerous attitude. Of course, it isn't a sin to take a few days off but making it a habit can spoil everything. This is the golden period to revise things that you may have forgotten with time.

When revising the course, you must stretch out your hands for help. There may be times when you may face trouble understanding certain topics. Teachers, parents, and tutors are always ready to help you. Taking help from specialists in a specific field will be a wise decision on your part.

Many students don't appreciate bowing down for guidance and assistance. Well, is this a matter of ego? Not really. It doesn't matter where you are today. Success is all about where the journey leads you to. Obstacles, complexities, and troubles are a part of this journey. You need to face all of these to emerge as a winner.

Sample Papers

Exam time is time to study. Your efforts should be to utilise each second of the day to gain knowledge. One of the best ways is to look for sample papers from the past and get an idea on the style of questionnaire and the complexities involved.

Preparing for examinations is no less than winning a battle. Apart from proper planning and ample time, one needs to stay calm and equipped with right arms in order to win this battle. When it comes to exams, sample papers from previous academic years will serve for the best tools here.

Solving sample papers will help you recognize your strengths and weaknesses. You get to know about the pattern of questionnaire paper and enhance your confidence to appear in these exams. When solving these papers, you need to take time into consideration. Keep a timer with you and try to solve the paper within the time period set.

Sample papers give you an idea on important topics, the time period allotted to solve papers, the questionnaire style, and a lot more. The idea is to follow a systematic method when preparing for exams. This will keep you away from unnecessary stress and anxiety during exams.

Studies have revealed that success mostly depends of strong will power and self-determination. One's confidence in intrinsic skills and capacity is instrumental in achieving success.

High Order Thinking

"The world as we have created it is a process of our thinking. It cannot be changed without changing our thinking."

–Albert Einstein

To achieve bigger things in life, we must dream big and think high. So, all those who aspire to be toppers should start developing high order thinking. I would like to quote an incidence to support this theory to inspire you think bigger, better, and higher.

Once I was enjoying a casual stroll at the India Gate with my friend, Veeru. Amidst the hustle bustle of the public place, we saw a Mercedes Benz approaching towards the entry point. A chauffeur dressed smartly in pristine white uniform got down and opened the rear door of the car. A man in his thirties proudly got down from the luxury vehicle and the driver smoothly drove the car away.

"Look at the driver! How lucky he is! A large part of his job involves roaming around in a luxury car," Veeru said to me.

"The driver?" I asked. "Did you just see the driver? The owner of the car is luckier! Well I don't blame you. It is your thought that makes you notice the driver. People who think higher and dream bigger are owners of these cars," I said.

"So, if I dream of owning a Benz, I will get it one day?" Veeru asked.

"Well, not exactly a luxury car, but you may own a Sedan! It's all about how big you think. But if you envy the fortune of that driver, you may not even own a two-wheeler," I explained.

Veeru wasn't convinced by the theory. So I had to explain him with some inspirational examples from the life of our honourable ex-president Shri Abdul Kalam Azad. He came from a poor background and started working at an early age to supplement his family's income. After completing school, Kalam distributed newspapers to financially contribute to his father's income. In his school years, he had average grades, but was described as a bright and hardworking student who had a strong desire to learn and spend hours on his studies, especially mathematics. His will power and high thinking helped him emerge as a great scientist and eventually the president of India.

Patience is the Key

Being a winner and accomplishing goals is on almost everybody's mind. But does everybody come across as successful person? No. Why? The reason is lack of passion and the determination to stand out and actually fulfil dreams. Dreaming about being a topper is easy but taking steps towards winning is what matters more. Strong determination and patience are major elements that distinguish toppers from rest of the crowd.

Being a topper is no child's play. One needs to have an eye of an expert to recognise valuable things. Being an expert will help you win the best. Since the competition today is stiff, one needs to make efforts to be different and better than the rest to be a topper. So studying the way mediocre do can be detrimental for your ambition.

The path that takes you to success isn't easy. You may have to face a lot of troubles and difficulties during the journey. Patience and determination is necessary to tackle all kinds of negativities that one comes across when aspiring to become a topper.

Out of League

Success is better achieved with 'out of league' preparation. Rehearsing ahead of time will keep you calm when things get intense. Things turn out the best, for the people who make the best of how things turn out.

Toppers are different from mediocre. They do things losers don't want to do. Most mediocre students see gain while toppers see the gain in their mission. For toppers, winning is an attitude that keeps them going regardless of what happens. They may get tired and burnt out but nothing makes them lose hope.

Most importantly, toppers aren't the part of crowd. They are unique and follow a path that others don't dare to tread on.

Keep a Record of Helpful Sources

Toppers have secrets that help them win each battle they undertake. One of these secrets is that they keep a record of and hold on to helpful sources. Yes, toppers don't burn bridges because they know it is possible to cross the same river many times in life. So make sure you keep a record of those who would be helpful to you and guide you towards your goal.

Knowledge is power. The more you get the better. Interestingly, you can borrow it from anyone around you without the fear of returning it one day. So keep gathering knowledge whenever and wherever you get the chance to.

Tick Tock Tick – Give that Clock a Kick!

Moving at fast pace is what every student wants in the present time. However, this is not really possible as each individual is different and possesses varied levels of potential. Some students possess impressive grasping power and are surprisingly fast in learning various topics. Usually students with these qualities are known to be more successful. Hence, it is important to focus on finishing important tasks off with complete dedication.

A lot of students have a habit of keeping tabs on time. They keep on having a look at the clock while accomplishing a specific task. This is where they go wrong. Experts feel that one must look at the clock only when they had achieved a target for the day. The clock may prove to be a permanent lock to your door to success. So ditch the clock! Don't stop to know what time it is and do what it is built for – keep going!

Accept your Weaknesses

"Growth begins when we begin to accept our weaknesses."

- Jean Vanier

One of the greatest weaknesses of human beings is their inability to accept weaknesses. All of us try to ignore our weaknesses and avoid sharing them with people. In fact, we have problems when others acquaint us with these shortcomings.

Unless we accept our weaknesses, it isn't possible to work towards removing them. It is as simple as the theory that one shouldn't hide anything from a doctor. Regardless of the number of problems one faces, one must provide complete details for the same to the health care practitioner. This will help him prescribe effective medications and treatment. Hiding things can be detrimental to one's own health.

Kabir had once said – "One who acquaints you with your weaknesses should be considered as a true friend as they hold the power to know what dwells deep within us."

Students should be their own critics. The moment they hear about or realise a weakness within, they should accept them and try to improve.

There are times when students waver and don't want to study. They just wish to get out of the whole preparation thing. However, this is just an ephemeral phase which will die a natural death. You must stay focus on your goals and make dedicated efforts to achieve them. When trying to become a topper, none of the goals in your life should be bigger than your desire to emerge as a winner. Once you have tried really hard, it is time to leave the rest to the Supreme Power.

Healthy Diet and Sound Sleep

Students tend to ignore their diet while preparing for exams. They don't get enough sleep. Teachers, experts in the field of education, and doctors recommend at least 6-7 hours of uninterrupted sleep for students. According to researchers, it is important to revise the subjects before hitting the sack. It enhances one's memory power and concentration.

Diet, according to health care practitioners, is an important aspect of student's life. Lack of proper nutrition can lead to several health problems. Just as a finely-tuned racing car, your body needs the right fuel (food) to achieve its true health potential. Nothing is more important than healthy eating! Put in the wrong fuel or less than what is required and it will refuse to deliver its full power and performance. In short, lack of a well balanced nutritional diet will make your body's engine cough, splutter, and eventually stall.

Health experts recommend students to include a lot of fresh fruits, vegetables, and juices in their regular dietary regime. One must stay away from junk food, fried snacks, and caffeine.

Here are some more tips to help you become a Topper.

Top Tips

- Just as all good things in life, the designation of being a topper comes with a price – 'Hard work'.
- To achieve success in future, one must learn from mistakes made in the past and focus on present.

- Each failure teaches you the secret for success.
- Being in a cool composed state is important for any student to achieve his or her goals. Iron is at its strongest best when cold.
- When encountered with trouble, seek guidance from seniors or experienced professionals such as professors, teachers, mentors. You may even consult your friends or parents.
- Regardless of how well you have prepared for exams, it is important to keep memorising, revising, and analysing course books until the examinations are over.
- The key to success is to solve ten questions at least once than solving one question ten times.
- Once a student is determined to be a topper, he will become one sooner or later.
- The word impossible is found only in the dictionary of fools. The wise person sets a goal and work hard to achieve it.

❑❑❑